A FRANCISCAN VIEW
OF CREATION

LEARNING TO LIVE
IN A
SACRAMENTAL WORLD

ILIA DELIO, O.S.F.

VOLUME TWO
THE FRANCISCAN HERITAGE SERIES

CFIT/ESC-OFM
2003

© The Franciscan Institute
St. Bonaventure University
St. Bonaventure, NY 14778
2003

This pamphlet is the second in
The Franciscan Heritage Series
sponsored by the
Commission on the Franciscan Intellectual Tradition
of the English-speaking Conference of the
Order of Friars Minor
(CFIT/ESC-OFM)

General Editor
Joseph P. Chinnici, O.F.M.

Assistant Editor
Elise Saggau, O.S.F.

ISBN
1-57659-201-4

Library of Congress Control Number
2003106067

Printed and bound in the United States of America
BookMasters, Inc.
Mansfield, Ohio

TABLE OF CONTENTS

GENERAL EDITOR'S INTRODUCTION

On behalf of the Commission for the Retrieval of the Franciscan Intellectual Tradition (CFIT), I present to you with great pleasure this second volume of The Franciscan Heritage Series—*A Franciscan View of Creation* by Ilia Delio, O.S.F. The purpose of this volume, building on the general introduction established in our first publication, is to elucidate in greater detail the theology of creation as a foundational starting point for contemporary belief and practice. The centrality in our faith tradition of the relationship between the Creator and all of creation and the reflection of the Trinity's glory in everything that is, so fundamental to the spiritual vision of Francis and Clare, is now undergoing a renaissance in our twenty-first-century world. The present volume provides a fine stimulus for further reflection on this most important area.

Dr. Ilia Delio, O.S.F., a member of the Franciscan Servants of the Holy Child Jesus, North Plainfield, New Jersey, is presently at Washington Theological Union (WTU), Washington, D.C., serving as an associate professor of ecclesial history and Franciscan studies. She is a member of CFIT and director of the Franciscan Center at WTU, where she coordinates an annual symposium on Franciscan theology. A recognized scholar on the thought of St. Bonaventure, Dr. Delio here traces the theme of God and creation from the time of the conversion of Francis through the first century of Franciscan life and thought which culminated in the work of John Duns Scotus.

It is our hope that readers will take this short work and, with careful and thoughtful study, perhaps under the guidance of a mentor, begin to plumb the spiritual depths of our inheritance and comprehend the important uniqueness of its intellectual expression. Through reflection, prayer, conversation and action may we also explore these theological themes as they might be expressed in preaching, pastoral practice, the works of evangelization and community formation with friars, sisters and laity.

This present work takes its place within the context of a much larger Franciscan Heritage Series, which we hope will encompass topics such as the Iconography of the Crucified, Christian Anthropology, Ecclesiology, Scriptural Themes, Evangelization, History, moral decision making, the Natural Sciences, the Arts and other areas of contemporary concern. As further volumes develop, we hope also to include some of the many different carriers of our Franciscan Tradition—not just Francis and the cleric theologians, but also Clare, the women penitents and the laity.

Before our readers begin to enjoy the music of creation as it flows forth from the fullness of a Triune God, however, we must briefly indicate, in this Introduction, the origins of the Heritage Series, its relationship to a major initiative in the English-speaking world, and its connections with some significant trajectories in the social and ecclesial experience of the brothers and sisters of the thirteenth-century foundational period of the Franciscan family.

The Franciscan Intellectual Tradition Project

In March 2001, the English-speaking Conference, Order of Friars Minor, undertook an initiative for the contemporary retrieval of the Franciscan Intellectual Tradition. Composed of the leaders of the provinces and other entities of England, Ireland, Canada and the United States, the Conference established an inter-obediential commission to facilitate the coordination and networking of various publications and popular initiatives that were already taking place throughout the English-speaking world in the various countries which were represented. As one its first initiatives, this Commission for the Retrieval of the Franciscan Intellectual Tradition (CFIT) composed and published a strategic five-year plan, the purpose of which has been detailed in the General Editor's Introduction to Volume One of this Heritage Series. (See Kenan Osborne, OFM, *The Franciscan Intellectual Tradition: Tracing Its Origins and Identifying Its Central Components*, [St. Bonaventure, NY: Franciscan Institute Publications, 2003], vi-viii).

The Commission decided very early that one of its first major tasks would be to identify the central themes and emphases of the Franciscan Intellectual Tradition, particularly as that was embodied in key theological issues. We decided to begin on the theological level as we felt that the Tradition first took on its specific contours in this area and that theological reflection might provide the clearest orientation for our contemporary mission in Church and society. The Commission also recognized, however, that the Franciscan Tradition is rich in insights as to how the Christian message might intersect with the fields of politics, economics, psychology, sociology and environmental studies. Its own work would simply be complementing many other initiatives being undertaken in the wider Franciscan family, for example, among the many colleges and universities working to mainstream their inherited Franciscan charism.

After an initial theological synthesis that was published along with the Strategic Plan in a booklet entitled *The Franciscan Intellectual Tradition Project* (June 2001, available from the Franciscan Institute, St. Bonaventure, New York), two significant initiatives were immediately undertaken. The first was the publication of the proceedings of the annual symposium on Franciscan theology at the Washington Theological Union. This gathering is designed to interface, at a high scholarly level, the major theological themes of the Tradition with contemporary issues. Two publications represent the first efforts to make these insightful reflections available: *The Franciscan Intellectual Tradition* (St. Bonaventure, NY: The Franciscan Institute, 2002) and *Franciscan Identity and Postmodern Culture* (St. Bonaventure, NY: Franciscan Institute Publications, 2003). Subsequent volumes will address Creation, the Church, and Biblical Foundations.

The development and publication of a series of pamphlets entitled The Franciscan Heritage Series is the second major initiative. This Series has a different audience in mind and is pitched at a level different from the Washington Theological Union symposia essays. The Heritage Series is designed to make available to college teachers, preachers, formation directors, pastoral workers, and lay persons associated with the Franciscan movement some of the basic themes dominant in our Intellectual Tradition. The character of these offerings is less academic. While they presuppose some training in philosophy and theology, they try, as much as possible, to keep scholarly references to a minimum and to avoid the technical language associated with medieval scholasticism. Although each is complete in itself, no one volume is fully expository. In the long run, we hope that the compilation of multiple volumes will enable the lively student to grasp the Intellectual Tradition in its totality.

The Second Volume

In this context, the purpose of this second volume in the Series is threefold :

(1) To elaborate on the fundamental theme of "The Sacred Book Called Creation" as that was identified in the first volume in this Heritage Series by Kenan B. Osborne, *The Franciscan Intellectual Tradition, Tracing Its Origins and Identifying Its Central Components* (Franciscan Institute Publications, 2003).

(2) To illustrate the deep exchange which exists in our Tradition between experience, praxis and thought, between spirituality and theology, shown so clearly in Dr. Delio's reflections on *pietas, cortesia,* the prayer of the *Canticle, haecceitas* and "Creation as Beloved." The implications of this unified vision are indicated clearly in the conclusion, "What is Ours To Do."

(3) To establish an initial theological base from which our readers can see connections between the Franciscan Tradition and contemporary modes of thinking in science, physics and environmental studies.

We recognize that readers of this pamphlet may find some of its insights either too difficult to grasp or perhaps too simplified; yet other insights will be stimulating and encouraging. The author has included some helpful references in her endnotes. We hope that some teachers and practitioners will translate the basic themes presented in this volume into still more popular forms and make them accessible to an ever-wider public of interested parties. CFIT would like to sponsor two-page summaries and updates, in printed and web-page format, which might help form preaching, meditation and community conversation, and serve as an even more practical illustration of basic principles. Each person and each "community of learning" has a different role to play in the larger project. May the Lord, in an ever-deeper fashion, show each of us a way to make these profound insights and truths life-giving in our Church and society.

Making Connections

Many people associated with the Franciscan family live on a very practical and pastoral level. We are called to engage our neighbor in following the footprints of Our Lord and the way of Francis and Clare. The vision, after all, begins with an encounter with a leper and the making of mercy; in its very simplicity it reveals the "sweetness of God." In our work and in our daily lives, we are comfortable with this dimension of God's presence revealed in the ordinary. Our spirits resonate when Dr. Delio begins her reflections on creation by first examining Francis's own conversion as that was plumbed in the biographical traditions of Celano and Bonaventure. We see the connections between experience, prayer and language, when she returns to Francis's own words in her analysis of *The Canticle of Creatures* and refers to the poetry of Hopkins to capture Scotus's spiritual vision.

However, we may also find that the intellectual formulations of Bonaventure and Scotus in their *Sentence* commentaries are quite abstract and removed from everyday concerns, lacking in application. The technical language of scholasticism may be difficult for many of us. In addition, the hagiographers amongst us are well aware of the mutation that occurred in the image and experience of Francis as that was communicated from generation to generation. We know that historians have analyzed the institutional growth of the Franciscan family, its entrance into the medieval centers of learning and its removal from the popular base of Francis's own life and from his "conversion to poverty."

On a very intuitive, unconscious and popular level, we may approach the academic proponents of the Franciscan Vision with a prejudice. Our educational pedagogy may have taught us to separate the insights derived from ordinary experience from the insights of academic theology, the inspiration and intuition of Francis from the institutional work of Bonaventure and the philosophical-theological vision of Scotus, the formation experience of novitiate from the school experience of preparation for ministry, the educational experience of theology from the preaching and praxis of the parish and soup kitchen. The separation itself has been encouraged by broader intellectual developments in society and theological and institutional developments in the Church.

CFIT believes that these are lamentable divisions, ones that need particular healing in this contemporary era. It hopes to deal with the historical continuities and discontinuities in our Franciscan Tradition in a later volume. For the present, it is enough to note that while the language of scholastic theology may seem one step removed from experience, its carriers emerged from a communal and formational base steeped in the spiritual-theological vision of Francis and in the biographical and liturgical reflections of his early successors. Underneath the changing languages lies a profound spiritual continuity. The members of CFIT want our Franciscan way of life in the Church and in the world to be whole—a way of looking at the world and a way of believing that can animate our acting, our feeling and our thinking. The Heritage Series is a small attempt in the contemporary world to help bridge some gaps between our Franciscan experience of life and our intellectual formulations, between our personal longings and our public languages, between our spirituality and our theology. Dr. Delio's work goes a long way towards helping us develop an integrated vision, one that is able to combine experience and reflection, science and faith.

For example, we note, in this second volume of the Heritage Series, the strong link between the conversion of Francis and the conversion of thought demanded of the students in the academic expression of Franciscan theology in the early schools at Paris and Oxford. It might help readers envision the unity that CFIT is trying to foster if this unity can be seen as emerging from the intersection between

1. the challenges that Francis faced in the Church and society of his time, his social location;

2. his own Gospel experience as elucidated in his writings in response to the social and ecclesial challenges;

3. the different languages in which this has been communicated over time.

Let us briefly consider in an interpretive and reflective way each of these.

1. The *challenges of social location* faced by Francis of Assisi are in many ways similar to our own. To some extent these challenges gave birth to his particular emphasis on God-as-Creator and the sacramentality of everything that exists. Simply put, Francis was born into a world that, in some respects, had forgotten what it means to be both human and Christian. In reference to the theme of Creation, two particular social challenges can be noted: violence and suffering.

Myriad forms of social, political, cultural and ecclesial violence penetrated the experience and structures of Francis's day: a sustained refusal to heed the public laws, divisive political associations, popular incitements to riot, the destruction of property, armed insurrections against the institutional and personal symbols of public order (government buildings, castles, churches, classes of people), physical attacks, rivalries between families, contentious parties within the Church, daily arguments, abusive interpersonal behaviors, violations of human dignity by those with religious and political power over others, murder, and the daily assaults occasioned by the sometimes hostile natural forces of fire, wind and water, and the always hostile realities of hunger, sickness and death. (See Lauro Martines, ed., *Violence and Civil Disorder in Italian Cities 1200-1500* [Berkeley, 1972]). *This experience of violence and discord cannot be underestimated and the spiritual-emotive responses of dissension, suspicion, fear, disgust, hopelessness, revulsion, dissociation, envy and anger entered into the human heart through the processes of familial, cultural, social and ecclesial osmosis.* We see this reality reflected very clearly in the Rules of Francis and Clare with their admonitions against dissension, quarreling, arguing and judging, and their pleas to practice courtesy, mercy, respect and love of enemies (LR 3:10; RCl 10:4). It is implied as a backdrop in Francis's reference to "priests of this world" (Test 7). Only from such a context can the full depth of the passages from the *Later Admonition and Exhortation* be appreciated: "And let us love our neighbors as ourselves. And if anyone does not want to love them as himself, let him at least not do them any harm, but let him do good" ((2LtF 26-27).

This pervasive experience of violence and the knowledge of human complicity in sin were accompanied by great suffering. On an experiential level, the social and ecclesial environment itself called into question the goodness of human relationships, the beauty of creation, the sacramentality of the Church, the value of human existence. The very world and institutions that were to be carriers of life seemed to many to be complicit in a "culture of death." Why so much suffering? Where was God in the midst of it? Did God really create this world? And if so, was God good? Was there no place to rest one's weary head, no place of human mediation of the divine, no beauty in a disfigured world? Given such an atmosphere, it was no wonder that people gravitated to a narrative explanation of human life, a Cathar myth, as Delio expounds it, that could account for evil and suffering by defining the body as a cruel prison, matter as a carrier of death, the sacraments of the Church with their use of bread, water, wine, oil and physical touch as useless, and life in this world, body and blood, sexual relationships, the passage of time, earthly existence itself as diabolic tricks, cruel hoaxes of entrapment. Perhaps the Judaeo-Christian story of origins, the narrative of Genesis 1 in which God saw that "it was good," the great story of history captured in the opening of John's Gospel, "through the Word all things were made," and the story of the breaking of the Lord's body and the spilling of his blood were in actuality a narrative of the lie. How was one to interpret the worship of the Lord "in spirit and in truth"?

2.   Into this world, into its suffering truth and through the Spirit who hovered over its chaos at the beginning, the Lord led Francis of Assisi *to do penance, to work and to discover "sweetness."* And thus it has been for succeeding generations of Franciscans. Francis encountered God in the condition of being a creature, even in a leprous condition that was most disfigured, in a condition of violation and poverty, in the condition of God-with-us, Emmanuel, in the condition of a disfigured but grace-filled Church. He began to work with his hands, as did his Master, to become "simple and subject to all," to imitate as a co-worker a Creator who made all things, saw all things as good, redeemed all things and would bring all things to their transformation (ER 23). He began to preach and to live an "evangelism of the good," a life that affirmed the presence of grace in all things "visible and invisible." Being with the Church, he worked to assimilate into his whole life the opening creedal statement of the Fourth Lateran Council. He began to see, and, in the great liturgical tradition of the Judaeo-Christian heritage, he prayed:

Praise the Lord because He is good;
All you who read this, bless the Lord.
All you creatures, bless the Lord.
All you birds of heaven, praise the Lord.
All you children, praise the Lord (ExhP 9-13).

Francis took up in love the cross of his own suffering body and the cross of his neighbor's suffering body. From the widespread frame of Creation, which embraced all things, he worked for reconciliation. In so doing, he took into himself the groans also of "the whole created world as it eagerly awaits the revelation of the sons of God" (Rom. 8:19). He found himself called to follow the path of the Incarnate Lord, present from the beginning, who did not disdain to be born in the fullness of time, labor along the way and die.

From this One, Francis drew life. He grew in this experience of God as Creator of "everything spiritual and corporal," everything composed of matter, contingent and temporal. He grew in this experience of God-at-the-foundation-of-things and God-with-us to develop a praxis of affirming the created world. He began to be not repelled by the condition of being a creature but inspired by its beauty, its creative power, its dependency on the Creator, its capacity, because Creation itself is a grace and gives God glory by the mere fact of its existence and its goodness. Francis began to be energized by his mission to share in the movement of creation-redemption-completion. The way he himself governed began to be deeply related to how the earth nurtured human beings and how God governed the earth. Here was Francis's Gospel answer to the world's challenges and his Gospel "yes" to the world, the Church, his own human existence and that of his brothers and sisters. Here was a Gospel proclamation of *goodness at the heart of reality*.

3. With the help of others, Francis found a *language* to express this intuition about God as Creator and God-with-us. He did this in his prayers, his Creed, his sermons, his letters, his Rule, his evangelizing work and preaching, his symbolic texts of preaching to the birds, and his celebration of "the most Holy Body and Blood of our Lord Jesus Christ, in whom that which is in heaven and on earth has been brought to peace and reconciled to almighty God" (LtOrd 12-13). He left also for posterity the human and graced text of his own

life. Those who followed after the first brothers inherited this intuition, received these texts and the symbolic text of Francis's own stigmata—the transformation of his own matter into a sign of Christ. They confronted the problems of their times, and, in different languages (ones shaped both by their own university milieux and their own possibilities and constrained by their own communal disfigurements), tried to express this great vision of God-as-Creator and God-with-us.

In the course of history, the social location changed profoundly; yet we see in *A Franciscan View of Creation* the strong continuity in our Tradition between the spiritual vision of Francis's *Canticle of the Creatures* and its institutionalized and academic intellectual expression in Bonaventure and Scotus. Perhaps it is our task today to bridge the gaps that have developed between social location, spiritual experience, theology and practice. We know that we need to discover our own language; but first we must understand what our Tradition wishes to say and the different expressions it has taken.

The human reality and Gospel mission that challenged Francis of Assisi challenge us today. We too can surround ourselves and be complicit in patterns of personal and institutionalized violence. We see around us the attraction of narratives that address the problem of suffering by adopting a profound dualism, splitting the sacred from secular, the holy from the profane, the ordinary from the perfect, the above from the below, spirit from matter, God's presence from things that are created. And we find ourselves only partially equipped, as was the Church in Francis's day, to deal with these issues on an intellectual and practical level.

We have inherited not only the Creation vision of Francis, its expressions in the biographical and academic traditions of the first hundred years, but also a long history of the "death of nature," its de-sanctification, and, in the contemporary world, its exploitation. We have inherited a theology and moral praxis suspicious of science, a "thought style" which at times narrows the horizon and no longer centers mission in the panoramic vision of a God who is present in all things "spiritual and corporal." Our contemplative style has withdrawn us from the "contemplation of God in all things." Yet it is only from such a perspective that we can hope to engage with gentleness in processes of dialogue and inculturation.

We unconsciously participate in a rhetoric of the "no," which is always capable of identifying God's absence but rarely consistent in affirming God's presence in everything that is.

Embedded in this vision of Creation and communicated in our Franciscan Intellectual Tradition are implications for the world of politics, economics, social relations, family life, the Christian Catholic view of sexuality, environmental practice and daily human existence. Dr. Delio has pointed us in a direction. The real question is: Can we speak in the midst of our own social and ecclesial location a language of God-as-Creator and God-with-us, a language of life, a language of ritual, a language of social witness, a language of the intellect, a language of cooperation, dialogue and inculturation that for our own time will have us "do what is ours to do" in this Christian Catholic Franciscan way of Gospel Life? Such is the CFIT's purpose and hope in seeking companions on the way. May the reader beware!

Joseph P. Chinnici, OFM
Franciscan School of Theology
Berkeley, California
Good Shepherd Sunday, 2003

PART ONE
AUTHOR'S INTRODUCTION

T hough frightened for a moment by evolution, the Christian now perceives that what it offers is nothing but a
magnificent means of feeling more at one with God and
of giving oneself more to him. In a pluralistic and static Nature, the universal domination of Christ could, strictly speak-
ing, still be regarded as an extrinsic and super-imposed power.
In a spiritually converging world this "Christic" energy acquires an urgency and intensity of another order altogether. . .
. Christ invests himself organically with the very majesty of
creation. And it is in no way metaphorical to say that the human finds him/herself capable of experiencing and discovering
God in the whole length, breadth and depth of the world in
movement. To be able to say literally to God that one loves
him, not only with all one's body, all one's heart, all one's soul,
but with every fiber of the unifying universe—that is a prayer
that can only be made in space-time.

Pierre Teilhard de Chardin

I work as a secretary in Manaus, a large city in the Amazon
area of Brazil. When I step out of my apartment in the
morning, I step into a thick haze of smoke. My doctor tells
me that I have a serious respiratory infection from breathing
all this bad air. The papers tell us that the rainforest is burning
this year as it never did before. They say that in some places
even the lakes are on fire. We have had the worst drought in
twenty-five years, and this has caused many trees to dry out
and be vulnerable to fire. In addition, the government continues to pay people to slash and burn their land, cut down the
tropical trees, and use the land for farming. The farmers soon
find out that the soil lasts only several years, and then they
have nothing. But we never seem to learn. Now they tell me
that El Niño is going to bring even more droughts and make
things even worse. It is very discouraging.

Selena Casara, Manaus, Brazil

1

On Christmas Eve 1968, the first astronauts in orbit around the moon appeared live on television. Frank Borman read the opening verses of Genesis: "In the beginning God created the heavens and the earth. The earth was without form and void, and darkness was upon the face of the deep; and the Spirit of God was moving over the face of the water. And God said, 'Let there be light'; and there was light." Borman concluded his message with: "Greetings from the crew of Apollo 8. God bless all of you on the good earth." Borman and his crew were the first people to see the beauty of the earth as a blue and white gem spinning in the vastness of space, and the reading of Genesis seemed an appropriate response.[1] The photograph of the planet earth, reprinted in all the major magazines, triggered immense awe as people marveled at the tiny blue marble-like globe suspended in space. What could not be seen, however, was the excessive pollution and violence that has damaged and continues to damage the face of the earth. Nor could the astronauts' photograph capture the dynamism of the universe in which planet earth is embedded, an expanding, evolutionary universe, composed of millions of galaxies. The only visible beauty of the photograph was the picture of earth as a unified whole, as if a single note of music was written in the vast corners of space.

    Creation is a mystery. How it came into existence, why it is here are questions that scientists struggle to answer today. The Bible provides stories of creation that form the basis of Christian belief. It speaks of a Creator God and of harmony and order in the universe; however, it neither tells us how creation came into existence nor how it maintains its existence apart from its dependency on God. Because these questions intrigue both scientists and theologians alike, they comprise the basis of a lively discussion today in the areas of religion and science.

    Our intention here is not to examine the details of creation but to highlight insights from the Franciscan tradition on the meaning of creation and the relationship of humans to creation. Francis of Assisi has been known for centuries as a lover of nature and creatures. In 1980 Pope John Paul II named him patron saint of ecology. Francis's love for nature, however, grew out of a deep theological conviction that God is truly present to us in the Incarnation. The intimate link between creation and Incarnation is what marks the distinctively positive view of creation in the Franciscan tradition.

The purpose of this essay is to examine the Franciscan doctrine of creation. By exploring the role of creation in the life of Francis, as well as in the theology of Bonaventure and Scotus, we are able to address some of the important questions that confront us today such as: What is our fundamental relationship to nature? What is our role with regard to dominion "over" creation? What stance should we assume with regard to the ecological crisis in which we find ourselves? What is the meaning of Christian life in an evolutionary world? We may not be able to answer these questions entirely, but examining how Francis related to creation and how Bonaventure and Scotus viewed the significance of creation, we may come to a deeper appreciation of the Franciscan tradition we claim as our heritage.

PART TWO
FRANCIS OF ASSISI:
CREATION AS BROTHER/SISTER

I n a landmark essay, the historian Lynn White asserts that Christians are responsible for the ecological crisis because they took God's command to have dominion over creation (Gen. 1:27-28) as a command to dominate and subdue it. White argues that no religion has been more focused on humans than Christianity and none more rigid in excluding all but humans from divine grace and in denying any moral obligation to lower species.[2] We will continue to have an ecological crisis, he claims, until we reject the Christian axiom that nature has no reason for existence except to serve us.[3] White maintains that because the roots of the trouble are largely religious, the remedy must be essentially religious. He suggests that "the profoundly religious, but heretical, sense of the primitive Franciscans for the spiritual autonomy of all parts of nature may point a direction,"[4] and he proposes Francis as a patron saint for ecologists. His lament that Christians usurped the Genesis text for their own advantage is countered by his praise of Francis of Assisi whom he extols as the "democratic saint" of all creatures.[5]

Francis and His Milieu

Although White points to the Genesis text as the basis of our ecological crisis, it is precisely the biblical view of creation, with its belief in a divine creation organized according to a hierarchical and unchanging plan, that formed the basis of Francis's view of the natural world.[6] Francis obtained his terms and ideas on nature not from books or scientific studies but from the Bible, especially the psalms and canticles of the liturgical offices he recited daily.[7] Francis believed in the doctrine of creation with his whole heart. It told him that the entire universe—the self and the total environment to which the self belongs (microcosm and macrocosm)—is the product of the highest creative power, the creativity of transcendent love.[8] By creation God brings to being what did not exist and then in love lets it be itself. Consequently, Francis's belief in creation did not have a

5

constricting effect on him nor did it inhibit him in any way. On the contrary, it liberated him, which is precisely what genuine belief ought to do.[9]

Francis had a basic education in reading and writing in the local church school of Assisi. Since he had not been trained as an intellectual in his youth, he never absorbed the Christian Neoplatonic attitude toward creation. Neoplatonism was a hierarchical way of viewing God and the world and passed into the Middle Ages through the writings of Augustine and Pseudo-Dionysius, among others. The Neoplatonic ladder of ascent presented a movement away from, and rising above, natural, sensible things, as if they were inferior and, in some sense, not truly real.[10] The emphasis of spirit over matter according to a hierarchy of being meant an intellectualizing of mystical experience.[11] In this respect, the Neoplatonic tradition with its insistence on inner illumination and mental ascent diminished the natural goodness of the created world. Neoplatonists believed that the created world should motivate one to turn inward in the search for God. In order to know true reality, one had to transcend this earthly world and contemplate the spiritual world above. The Neoplatonists, therefore, turned quickly from the material world and its individual creatures to scale the metaphysical ladder to the spiritual and divine realms by means of universal concepts.[12]

Unlike the Neoplatonists who withdrew from the sensual world in order to contemplate God, Francis attained the heights of contemplation through his penetrating vision of creation. With a basic education in reading and writing, Francis came from a base of popular and lay experience. His family was part of the rising merchant class in Assisi. His father was a cloth merchant and owned a shop in Assisi where Francis apparently worked for some time. He was not only familiar with the daily business of buying and trading cloth but he came into contact with many different types of people—farmers, craftsmen, artists, bakers—people who worked with their hands and valued the material things of the earth. The idea of transcending this world to contemplate true reality, as the Neoplatonists maintained, would have been foreign to Francis's thinking. Rather, he regarded earthly life as possessing ideal, positive potential as God's creation. Some regard him as "the first materialist" in the best sense of the word because of the way he looked on the material world—not for *what* it is but for *how* it is—God's creation.[13]

Francis has been described as a nature mystic, one who finds God in the vast and beautiful fields of nature. A nature mystic is one whose mystical experiences involve an appreciation of creation as God's handiwork; nature manifests the divine. Francis's nature mysticism included a consciousness of God, with the appropriate religious attitudes of awe and gratitude.[14] His joyful attitude toward creation was a far cry from Neoplatonic speculative mysticism, which focused on an abstract cosmological structure. Rather, he took spontaneous joy in the material world, singing its praises like a troubadour poet. With a disarming sense of immediacy, he felt himself part of the family of creation.

Francis's love of creation was in opposition to the Cathars of his time, who maintained a split between matter and spirit. The town of Assisi where Francis grew up was influenced by the Cathar heresy. The name "Cathari," meaning "the pure ones," comes from the Greek term *katharos* or "pure."[15] These heretical dualists believed that matter was created by an evil god and spirit by a good god. The world in which humans live out their earthly life is evil.

One version of this heresy maintained that the material universe (including animals) is the creation of the first of the angels, one who rebelled against God and thus was expelled from paradise along with all those who participated in the rebellion. From Adam and Eve onward, the spiritual principles of the fallen angels were gradually incorporated into human beings. Humans thus became the prisons of the angels, who passed from one body to another by means of the sexual act. Then God, taking pity on the unfortunate human condition, sent Jesus, the angel closest to him, to earth to teach men and women the way of liberation. Jesus appeared incarnate through another angel, who took the form of the woman Mary. In human guise, Jesus preached the possibility of salvation.[16]

A second version of the same heresy asserted a strong dualistic concept. It held that there were two equal and clearly opposed principles, God and Satan, one at the head of the spiritual kingdom and the other at the head of the material kingdom. The latter succeeded in sending one of his creatures, camouflaged as an angel of light, to seduce the angels of the good god. The evil god, therefore, burst into the realm of light and led angelic persons away from the good god. Then, in the material world, the evil god forced spirits into corporate bodies as into a prison. The good god in turn permitted this as a punishment for their infidelity.[17] These heretics therefore held that there are two creators. The one who created invisible things they called the benevolent god; the one who created visible things they called the malevolent god. The New Testament they attributed to the benevolent god; the Old Testament they attributed to the malevolent god and rejected it altogether, except for certain authorities that are inserted into the New Testament from the Old and which, out of reverence to the New Testament, they esteemed worthy of reception.[18]

The Cathar heresy was immensely popular, especially throughout northern and central Italy and southern France. The popularity of this belief probably lay in the fact that medieval Europe experienced profound suffering on many different levels. In the area of Assisi, for example, lack of work, exploitation by those who assigned work, illness due to wars, famine and poor hygiene were common, especially among the people of lower rank. Catharism offered a path to salvation by escaping the evil of matter and entering into the realm of light through knowledge of the Gospels. Among the various strains of Catharism, denial of the crucifixion of Christ (as salvific) and resurrection of the body were prominent. Through the eyes of the Cathars, one could explain the suffering of this world as the result of an evil god. The question of evil in the world was, in Francis's time as in our own time, a difficult question to address. How do we affirm a good God in an evil world? Or, we might ask, is the world really evil? In Francis's time, the Cathars attempted to overcome the evil of the world through rituals of purification, withdrawal and strict ascetical practices, including abstinence from foods such as meat, eggs, milk and all other food produced by sexual union.[19] Their interpretation of the Gospel led to a denial of the world and the suffering within it.

The development of the Franciscan Intellectual Tradition is based on the fact that Francis's vision of creation differed from that of the Neoplatonists and that of the Cathars. While both of these traditions, on popular and mythological levels, led to a depreciation and suspicion of the world of matter, Francis's roots were in popular religiosity. His own conversion story, beginning with the experience of "sweetness" in the midst of the world and his premier focus on the humility of the Incarnation and charity of the Passion of Christ, led him to embrace matter as the locus for the encounter with Christ and God. His following of the Gospel led not to the denial of suffering but to the acceptance of it as the deepest sense of human existence. His conversion was centered on Christ in the crib, Christ on the way and Christ on the cross. The human suffering of God-with-us explained, illuminated and justified all human suffering.

It is true that Francis would carry certain tensions with him throughout his life, but the tensions themselves were indicative of his fundamental desire to follow the path of the One who became human for us. We can see the central point of his vernacular theology most clearly as it began to be developed in the biographical traditions of Celano and Bonaventure and thus entered into the consciousness of future generations and the academic stream of the Franciscan Intellectual Tradition.

The Conversion of Francis: The Biographical Traditions

Francis's conversion story in his *Testament* begins with doing mercy among the lepers. He describes it in this way: "That which was bitter became sweet." Thereafter, care for the lepers became the center of Francis's life and continual conversion.[20] The biographical traditions of Thomas of Celano and Bonaventure focused on this conversion story and its theological meaning through two significant popular images: the encounter with the Crucified in the church of San Damiano and the dramatic meeting with a single leper. According to the second life of Francis by Celano, Francis encountered the crucified Christ in the church of San Damiano where "the image of Christ crucified spoke to him. 'Francis, go rebuild my house; as you see, it is all being destroyed.'"[21] At first, Francis understood these words literally, since the church was dilapidated. He came to understand, however, that it was not a material building that Christ wanted repaired but rather the Church—his mystical body—and ultimately, we could say today, the body of all creation. In the crucifix at San Damiano, the suffering and glorified Christ was pictured as having redemptive value in the reality of human existence. Here was the only power able to give meaning and sense to human suffering because, in and through the suffering of Christ, the Christian encountered the overflowing love of God, the source of all creation and the power of our redemption. God has entered into the material world with all its sufferings and limitations in and through the person of Jesus Christ.

Bonaventure, in his *Major Legend of Saint Francis*, dramatizes Francis's conversion as narrated in the *Testament* by describing his encounter with a single leper. Up until his conversion, Francis had complete disdain for lepers and loathed the very sight of them. Around the time of his conversion, Francis met a leper one day along the road and, instead of turning away in disgust, he dismounted his horse, gave the leper alms and kissed his hand.[22] Through this image, Bonaventure communicates something very similar to what Celano had written about and Francis himself had described as an experience of "sweetness." Just as Francis realized that God has humbly bent over in love to embrace us in the humility of the Incarnation and in the charity of the Passion, so too he realized that the suffering of humanity and all creation could only be lifted up through solidarity in love.

The God of Francis of Assisi was not the God of the Cathars but the God of compassionate love, whom Francis encountered in the person of Jesus Christ. Face to face with the crucified and glorified Christ in the broken down church of San Damiano, Francis sought to respond to that love. He had discovered "sweetness" in the face of a creature composed of matter, and, by meeting the God of overflowing goodness in the person of Jesus Christ, Francis came eventually to realize God's goodness at the heart of all matter. He came to "see" that all creation is filled with the abundant goodness of God. The thirteenth-century Franciscan penitent, Angela of Foligno, captured this same truth in another startling image. In a vision she saw creation "pregnant with God" and she exclaimed:

> [I] beheld and comprehended the whole of creation, that is, what is on this side and what is beyond the sea. . . . And my soul in an excess of wonder cried out: "This world is pregnant with God!" Wherefore I understood how small is the whole of creation—that is, what is on this side and what is beyond the sea, the abyss, the sea itself, and everything else— but the power of God fills it all to overflowing.[23]

So too, we might say that Francis perceived creation to be "pregnant with God."

Coming to an awareness of God's presence in creation was not an immediate experience for Francis but required growth in love. Conversion is a slow, lifelong process. It is a constant effort of moving away from sin-centered attitudes and behaviors toward God-centered relationships. With this movement from sin toward God, there is a gradual change in one's consciousness or awareness of others and in one's relationship to others. It took Francis a lifetime to realize his integral relationship to others, not only to humans but to all of creation. The *Canticle of Creatures*, which sings of Francis's cosmic fraternity, his integral relationship to all the elements of the universe, was composed in 1225, one year before he died. It took Francis a lifetime to realize that he was truly brother to the sun, moon, stars, fire and water, that is, to the whole cosmos.

According to his biographer, Thomas of Celano, Francis aspired to be a knight but was wounded in battle and afterwards showed little appreciation for creation. Celano writes that, around the time of Francis's conversion,

> the beauty of the fields, the delight of the vineyards, and whatever else was beautiful to see could offer him no delight at all. He wondered at the sudden change in himself, and considered those who loved these things quite foolish.[24]

How did Francis change? How did he come to realize his intimate relationship to creation? Both Celano and Bonaventure claim that such a relationship came about through his loving relationship with Jesus Christ.[25] It is difficult to say exactly how Christ led Francis to discover an integral relationship to creation. Bonaventure highlights the bond of compassionate love between Francis and the crucified Christ in such a way that love alone seems to have transformed Francis into a friar minor. Although Bonaventure constructs a portrait of the saint through the lens of the crucified Christ, still he captures what is essential to the spirit of Francis, namely, the centrality of love. Love has the power to unite and transform. The heart, not pure reason, whispers that love is the greatest power for good in the universe. Love opens up the mystery at the heart of everything. The heart knows too that love is vulnerable; it leaves itself open to ridi-

cule and rejection, but it can never be conquered. The heart says: let
go and risk everything. In the moment of surrender, the self and the
cosmos become one.[26] With Francis, therefore, it is love that bound
him to the things of creation and opened his eyes to the truth of God
in creation. He came to realize that the Incarnation sanctifies all creation. In Jesus not only does the fullness of divinity reside, but in
him is subsumed all of creation as well. Earth, water, fire and air, the
four cosmic elements, are not just God's creation; they are made holy
by Jesus Christ, in whom the elements of the universe are further
sanctified. And as Jesus ascended to his true home in heaven, so all
of creation will ascend one day to become a new earth in a new
heaven.[27]

Through his passionate love of Jesus Christ, Francis embraced
all of creation as that which has been created by God's Word made
tangible in Jesus. Jesus himself is the Word that speaks creation and
redeems creation and summons all creation to join him in Paradise.
For St. Francis, therefore, everything is created through the Word
and is on its way forward to heaven, to the Garden of Innocence,
that garden described in the book of Genesis at the very beginning
of creation. The trouble is, we erroneously think that creation itself
is its own end, our heaven or paradise. Even the earth, which we
mistakenly believe to be our true home, is itself a pilgrim on its way
back to the Word who spoke it and redeemed it.[28]

Francis came to understand that all creation, like himself, is called
to give praise and glory to God. He lived in love, and, by loving
other creatures, let them be, encouraging them to grow in their
uniqueness, sharing with them their very being.[29] Everything spoke
to Francis of the infinite love of God. Trees, worms, flowers by the
side of the road—all were for him saints gazing up into the face of
God. Creation became the place to find God and, in finding God,
Francis realized his intimate relationship to all of creation.

The Family of Creation

In his *Major Legend*, Bonaventure describes Francis's relationship with
Christ as one of deepening piety. The word "piety" (*pietas*) means
"blood-related" or "family-related." It can be defined as an attitude
of respect toward those to whom one is bound by ties of religion,
consanguinity; of relationships between human beings.[30]

Bonaventure highlights the idea that, through his relationship with Christ, Francis came to realize his "family" relatedness to everything, including the tiny creatures of creation. "True piety," Bonaventure writes, "had so filled Francis's heart and penetrated its depths that it seemed to have claimed the man of God completely into its dominion. This is what, through devotion, lifted him up to God; through compassion, transformed him into Christ; through self-emptying, turned him to his neighbor; through universal reconciliation with each thing, refashioned him to the state of innocence."[31] Bonaventure contrasts the piety or family-relatedness of Francis to the attitude of the impious or of those who inflict cruelty on nature. Bonaventure describes, for example, how Francis cursed a vicious sow that had killed an innocent newborn lamb. The sow got sick and, after three days, died and was thrown into a ditch. Bonaventure comments:

> Let human *impiety* pay attention to how great a punishment might at least be inflicted on it, if such animal cruelty is punished with so horrible a death. Let also the devotion of the faithful weigh how the *piety* in God's servant was of such marvelous power and of such abundant sweetness that even the nature of animals acknowledged it in their own way.[32]

Francis's piety was the fruit of his ongoing conversion. Growing in union with Christ through the Spirit gave Francis a new relationship to new nature, one in which grace and innocence prevailed, not sin and conflict. The created world provided for him. Bonaventure recounts how Francis's thirst was once quenched by water from a rock.[33] His piety was the source of his reverence for animals and he recognized them as fellow creatures and signs of Christ. As Celano writes:

> That the bees not perish of hunger in the icy winter, he [Francis] commands that honey and the finest wine should be set out for them. He calls all animals by a fraternal name, although, among all kinds of beasts, he especially loves the meek.[34]

The notion of *cortesia* or deferential behavior characterized Francis's respect for creation, including the natural elements such as fire. He made use of chivalric values to express his unique ideas of spiritual honor and deference between all the levels of creation. Celano provides an example of *cortesia* by recounting the story of Francis's cauterization for an eye disease. To prepare the iron instrument for treatment, the physician had to place it in the fire until it became red hot. Francis apparently panicked and spoke to the fire:

> My brother fire, your beauty is the envy of all creatures, the Most High created you strong, beautiful and useful. Be gracious to me in this hour; *be courteous!* For a long time I have loved you in the Lord. I pray the Great Lord who created you to temper now your heart that I may bear your gentle burning.[35]

While we might find this deference toward nature exaggerated, Francis's respect for creation was not a duty or obligation but arose out of an inner love by which creation and the source of creation, namely God, were intimately united. All of creation was a means to contemplate the power, wisdom and goodness of the Creator. Celano writes:

> Even for worms he had a warm love, since he had read this text about the Savior: *I am a worm and not a man.* That is why he used to pick them up from the road and put them in a safe place so that they would not be crushed by the footsteps of passersby. . . . Whenever he found an abundance of flowers, he used to preach to them and invite them to praise the Lord, just as if they were endowed with reason.[36]

The life of Francis gave new meaning to the divine command of dominion found in Genesis 1:28. He did not consider himself at the top of a hierarchy of being nor did he declare himself superior to the non-human creation. Rather than being at the top rung of the ladder of creation, Francis saw himself as part of creation. His spirituality overturned the spirituality of hierarchical ascent and replaced it with a spirituality of descending solidarity between humanity and creation.[37] That is, instead of using creatures to ascend to God (in a transcending manner), he found God in all creatures and identified with them as a brother. Bonaventure writes: "He would call creatures, no matter how small, by the name of 'brother' or 'sister' because he knew they shared with him the same beginning."[38]

By surrendering himself and daring everything for love's sake, the earth became his home and all creatures his brothers and sisters. That led him to love and respect the world around him and in him and made him a truly humble person. Francis realized that the source of his own life was the very source of all created things and all that exists. He discovered, therefore, that the truth of his identity could not be found apart from the things of creation, including the tiniest of creatures. All things manifested to him the presence of God.

Incarnation and the Holiness of Creation

In and through his relationship with Jesus Christ, Francis came to realize that the entire creation is holy. Celano highlights this idea in his account of Francis's Christmas celebration in Greccio. It is here that the intimate link between creation and Incarnation became "visible." Francis wanted to show how God entered into our everyday world of creation through the Incarnation. At Greccio he set up a manger scene with hay and animals and had a small altar built over the manger to celebrate the Mass. As he stood in ecstatic prayer over the manger weeping tears of joy at the scene of the Incarnation, the whole creation responded in celebration. Celano writes: "The night is lit up like day, delighting both man and beast. . . . The forest amplifies the cries and the boulders echo back the joyful crowd. . . . The whole night abounds with jubiliation."[39] As Greccio became a new Bethlehem, Francis embraced the good things of creation as a brother embraces the members of his family.

Francis came to realize that it is Christ who sanctifies creation and transforms it into the sacrament of God. The intimate link between creation and Incarnation revealed to Francis that the whole of creation is the place to encounter God. As his eyes opened to the holiness of creation, he came to see that there is nothing trivial or worthless. Rather, all created things point beyond themselves to their Creator. Even two crossed twigs reminded him of the cross of Christ. Wherever he went for prayer, into lonely wooded valleys or fields or hollowed out caverns, he would bend low and kiss the ground saying, "We adore you Lord Jesus Christ here and in all your churches throughout the world for by your holy cross you have redeemed the world."[40]

Bonaventure claims that everything in creation "spoke" to Francis of God. He came to "see" God's goodness in every aspect of creation, so that everything ultimately led him to Christ, the Word of God. That Francis came to "see" God in creation points to the idea that Francis contemplated God in the things of creation. Contemplation is a penetrating gaze that gets to the truth of reality, and Francis came to "see" the truth of things by following the footprints of Jesus Christ. Bonaventure describes the contemplative vision of Francis as "contuition," that is, seeing things for what they truly are in God. In his *Major Legend* he writes:

> In beautiful things he [Francis] contuited Beauty itself and through the footprints impressed in things he followed his Beloved everywhere, out of them making for himself a ladder through which he could climb up and lay hold of him who is utterly desirable. . . . He savored in each and every creature that fontal goodness and . . . sweetly encouraged them to praise the Lord.[41]

These footprints of God impressed on the things of creation enabled Francis to find God wherever he went in the world, and finding God in the things of creation led him to the embrace of Jesus Christ, for Christ is the Word of God made visible in the world.

According to Bonaventure, Francis matured into a "state of innocence" by universal reconciliation with each thing through his union with Christ.[42] From earliest times, Christian teaching has pointed to Christ as the new Adam who restores, through obedience, the paradise that the first Adam lost through disobedience (cf. Rom. 5:12-21 and the two Adams). The saints, like Christ, are also the new Adam bringing about peace and harmony in creation. According to Francis's biographers, the creatures responded to his commands because the power of love had made him a brother to all of them.[43] The image of the new Adam plays out in Bonaventure's *Major Legend*. Bonaventure describes how Francis admonished sheep, blessed a fish and brought a flock of birds to obedience.[44] Francis found himself in a familial relationship with creation, calling out to "brother lamb" and "sister birds." Celano recounts how Francis once called a cricket over to him to sing: "My sister cricket, come to me! Sing, my sister cricket, and with joyful song praise the Lord your Creator!"[45] It seems that Francis's world was so imbued by the goodness of God that he was aroused by *everything* to divine love. Bonaventure writes: "Aroused by all things to the love of God, he rejoiced in all the works of the Lord's hands and from these joy-producing manifestations he rose to their life-giving principle and cause."[46] And Celano says: "Fields, vineyards, rocks and woods, and all the beauties of the field, flowing springs and blooming gardens, earth and fire, air and wind; all these he urged to love of God and to willing service."[47]

We may find in such harmony with nature either pure utopia or the imagination of Francis's biographers. However, what Francis attained in his life was a true sense of justice in creation. As he continued to move more deeply into the mystery of God through his relationship with Christ, he came to realize his familial relationship to creation. Realization of this enabled him to establish peaceful relationships with all creatures. For Francis, the kingdom of God is not in the future but already here and now through participation in it. His was a living out of the Gospel promise: "Repent and believe, for the kingdom of God is at hand" (Mt. 4:17). His life shows us that the justice and peace we hope and long for will not come about unless we are converted and strive for transformation in Christ. Peace is the fruit of justice. It is the order of love that flows from right ordered relationships. The Edenic relationships Francis came to share with all creatures emerged from his sense of justice. They signify that justice and peace are related to poverty, compassion, contemplation and on-going conversion by which we realize our familial bonds with all living creatures, joining with them on the journey into God.

The Canticle of Creatures

Through their biographies, both Celano and Bonaventure communicate in images and stories the sense of family that Francis attained with creation. For them the words "brother" and "sister" were words of mystery for Francis, so graphically did they disclose to him the structure of reality. By describing Francis's conversion in these terms, the biographies remained profoundly rooted in Francis's own vision as described in his *Canticle of the Creatures*. It would be appropriate then to conclude this section by returning to Francis's own words.

The *Canticle of the Creatures* is a hymn of praise that recapitulates Francis's journey to God in and through the beautiful things of creation. For Francis all of creation became a theophany, a manifestation of the goodness of God. But the *Canticle* also represents a lifetime of conversion, as Francis strove to be a brother to all things and to praise God in the cloister of the universe despite his sufferings, feelings of abandonment and darkness. In the *Canticle*, composed one year before he died and while he was lying ill in a small dark hut near San Damiano, Francis sang of the human family (brother-sister-mother) as the model for all relationships. The *Canticle of the Creatures* is the capstone of his theological vision. In this hymn, which celebrates the cosmic Christ, Francis addresses the "Most High," the ineffable God who has become flesh.[48] He alludes to the mystery of Jesus Christ through the metaphor of "Brother Sun." The words "Most High" and "humility," which begin and end the *Canticle*, symbolically enclose the whole universe in a cosmic Incarnation.[49] It is "Brother Sun" who is "the day and through whom [God] gives us light," who is at the center of the cosmos, who is the light that reveals the splendor and glory of the Father. Francis's praises of God are notes of joy resounding throughout the universe. He sings:

Praised be You, my Lord,
through Sister Moon and the stars,
in heaven You formed them
clear and precious and beautiful.
Praised be You, my Lord, through Brother Wind,
and through the air, cloudy and serene,
and every kind of weather,
through whom You give sustenance to Your creatures.
Praised be You, my Lord, through Sister Water,
who is very useful and humble
and precious and chaste.
Praised be You, my Lord, through Brother Fire,
through whom You light the night,
and he is beautiful and playful and robust and strong.
Praised be You, my Lord,
through our Sister Mother Earth,
who sustains and governs us, and who produces various
fruit with colored flowers and herbs.[50]

Like the three youths in the fiery furnace (Dan. 3:57-90), Francis praises God "through" (*per*) the elements of creation, for the *Canticle* discloses Francis's view of nature as a sacramental expression of God's generous love. This love binds us together in a family of relationships that are rightly termed "brother" and "sister." Francis acquired a "vision" of cosmic interdependency in and through his relation to Christ. Through his love of Christ crucified, he came to see the truth of reality, namely, that nothing exists autonomously and independently; rather everything is related to everything else. The *Canticle* expresses Francis's interior life transformed in Christ and projects that interior life onto the cosmos where Christ is the center of reality.[51] The *Canticle* is like a cosmic liturgy in which Christ is the high priest. Through him, with him and in him, everything is offered up in praise to the glory of the Father, in the love of the Holy Spirit.[52] Thus, just as Christ became the center of Francis's own life, so too Francis realized that Christ is the center of creation. All things are related to Christ as to their "brother." And because all things are united in Christ, one who lives in Christ finds oneself united to all things.

The *Canticle* reminds us that we humans are as dependent on the elements of creation as they are dependent on us. With his marvelous respect for creatures of all kinds, for sun, moon, stars, water, wind, fire and earth, Francis came to see that all creation gives praise to God. Brother Sun and Sister Moon praise God just by being sun and moon.[53] We might say that Francis became sensitive to the goodness of creation so that he came to understand, hear and see the sun and moon praising God. The *Canticle* foreshadows the new creation where we will find ourselves related to all things of creation in a spirit of reconciliation and peace.[54] It brings to our awareness that the entire creation is charged with the goodness of God so that, even in eternal life, creation will offer praise and glory to the Most High.

As the final song of his life, the *Canticle* reveals to us Francis's deep reflection on the mystery of the Incarnation. For Francis, it is the Incarnation that gives insight into the goodness of the created world as the sacrament of God. Creation and Incarnation are intimately united in such a way that we cannot truly grasp our relationship to creation apart from understanding our relationship to Jesus Christ. Francis's relationship to Christ did not follow a narrow path but grew to the widest possible horizon. The deeper he grew in relationship with Christ, the more he found himself intimately related to the things of creation as brother. We might say that his relationship with Christ changed his internal focus. He developed a deeper consciousness of "relatedness" and came to realize he was related to all things no matter how small, because everything shared in the primordial goodness of God, the source of his own life. Francis discovered that he was part of the cosmic family of creation.

While it was Christ who enabled Francis to see the truth of reality, namely, that everything is imbued with the goodness of God, it is how Francis lived in Christ that shaped his relationship to creation. Penance, poverty, humility and compassion were the values that forged Francis into a "cosmic brother," one who was related to all creatures and to the elements of creation. Through penance he recognized his sinfulness and need for conversion. Through poverty he became aware of the human tendency to possess as he realized his radical dependency on all things. Through humility he realized his solidarity with all creatures. Through compassion he came to have deep feelings for the things of the earth, including the tiniest of creatures. Francis became the "saint of ecology" not only because he loved nature but because he perceived the interrelatedness of creation with Christ as center. He came to realize that the world is the cloister, the place to find God, the One who is both present in every detail of the universe and, yet, infinitely transcendent and ineffable. Creation became a ladder by which he could ascend to God, not by transcending creation but by embracing it as brother. For by embracing the good things of creation, Francis came to embrace the whole Christ who is the Word of the Father.

PART THREE
BONAVENTURE'S
THEOLOGY OF CREATION

W hile Francis entered into the heart of creation by entering into the heart of Christ, the theologian, Bonaventure, reflected on the experience of Francis and developed a theology of creation that is both faithful to Francis's intuitions and to the Christian theological tradition itself. There is no doubt that Bonaventure reflected deeply on the life of Francis. As seventh Minister General of the Order, he strove to understand the meaning of being both Christian and Franciscan.

Scholars have pointed to a correlation between Bonaventure's thought and his birthplace, Bagnoregio. Situated in the Etruscan country about sixty miles north of Rome between Viterbo and Orvieto, Bagnoregio is perched high on the crest of a spur of land jutting into the Tiber valley. About seven miles to the west lies Lago di Bolsena, a deep blue lake that shines like a jewel in the crater of an extinct volcano. On its eastern slope, this volcano stretches in a plateau, which, after several miles, divides into what appear to be fingers of land separated from each other by deep gorges. Extending towards the Tiber, these fingers break off abruptly into the valley below.

Bagnoregio is built along the thin edge of one of these fingers. Scanning the horizon, the visitor has a breathtaking sense of the vastness of space—deep gorges plunging down on each side, massive cliffs rising across the gorges, directly ahead the steep drop off into the Tiber valley and in the distance lofty mountains in the direction of Todi. This setting easily awakens a sense of joy in nature—of awe at its power and at the same time peace and harmony. Bagnoregio seems to be the midpoint of a vast and ordered cosmos, the center of the earth as it were; for it lies on a pinnacle of land rising from the valley, ringed about by a sweeping circular horizon whose outlines are traced by massive mountains.[55]

Although little is known about Bonaventure's early years in Bagnoregio, we can see how this landscape could have shaped his vision. In the sweeping landscape of this unusual place, there is a natural resonance with the distinctive elements of his thought. As the town now stands, it is a powerful symbol of one of the principal metaphors of Bonaventure's theology and spirituality, that is, the symbol of the circle with its circumference and center.[56] God can be thought of as "an intelligible sphere," he wrote, "whose center is everywhere, and whose circumference is nowhere."[57]

As a friar Bonaventure, like Francis, recited the psalms that praised God for the works of his hand and the wonders of creation. However, he also studied at the University of Paris where he learned about the exemplary world of Augustine, the sacramental vision of the Victorines and the self-diffusive goodness of Pseudo-Dionysius. These thinkers helped shape Bonaventure's understanding of creation and the God-world relationship. As a Franciscan and a theologian, he translated Francis's vernacular theology into scholastic theology without losing the distinct characteristics of Francis's spirituality.[58] He distilled the essence of Francis's intuitions into a theological *vision* that holds immense relevance for us today.

Creation: A River and Song of the Trinity

Bonaventure's theology of creation takes as its starting point the Trinity of love. In the first book of his commentary on the *Sentences*, he writes that creation is like a *river* that flows from a spring, spreads throughout the land to purify and fructify it, and eventually flows back to its point of origin.[59] This image not only speaks to us of Bonaventure's appreciation for the beauty of creation but it also indicates that he saw the deep intimate relationship between creation and the triune God. It is an image that imparts to creation a vibrancy of life replete with the self-diffusive goodness of God. Creation flows from the fountain fullness, the *spring* of the creative and dynamic Trinity.

Bonaventure describes creation as sharing in the mystery of the generation of the Word from the Father. It is a limited expression of the infinite and dynamic love between the Father and Son. It emerges out of this relationship and explodes into "a thousand forms" in the universe.[60] Bonventure uses the term "emanation" (*emanatio*)[61] to describe the birth of creation from the womb of the triune God of love. Although the platonic use of this term means that creation necessarily flows out of the infinite, transcendent One, Bonaventure uses the term "emanation" in a Christian context. Creation, he writes, is like a beautiful *song* that flows in the most excellent of harmonies. It is a song that God *freely* desires to sing into the vast spaces of the universe.[62] There is nothing that compels God to create. Rather, creation is simply the finite loving outflow of an infinitely loving God. God *desires* to create because God is love, and perfect love can never be self-contained but must be shared freely with another. The world exists, Bonaventure indicates, by virtue of the free creative power of divine love. Creation is a free act of divine goodness spilling forth from the infinite divine community of love.

To say that creation flows out of the infinite fountain of divine self-diffusive goodness is to say that God is creative and loving. The divine Word is the *Art of the Father* because the Word expresses all the divine ideas (of the Father). When that Word is uttered in time, the canvas of creation unfolds. The triune God is then revealed as a divine Artist, and creation is the finite expression of the Artist's infinite ideas. As a work of art, creation is intended to manifest the glory of the *Artist-Creator*. In order for divine glory to be consciously expressed, God creates human beings who are capable of participating in and manifesting that glory.[63] A world that manifested the glory of God but did not include some creature able to perceive and revel in that glory would make little sense. In fact, such a world might suggest a selfish or a self-centered God.[64] But, indeed, this is not the case. Rather, God freely creates a glorious universe and calls forth within this universe human persons who are endowed with the freedom to participate in this divine artistic splendor.

The Order and Harmony of Creation

The beauty of creation on which Bonaventure reflected was evident in the order and harmony of the things of creation.[65] The beauty, order and harmony of creation signified to Bonaventure that this created world is not simply a stage for human activity or a backdrop to human longings, but that the whole of creation has meaning and purpose. It comes from God, reflects the glory of God and is intended to return to God.[66] Creation, we might say, is like a cosmic symphony. Bonaventure's vision of creation, with its emphasis on harmony and order, was compatible with the Ptolemaic universe in which he lived. Such a closed universe, unlike the evolutionary one we know today, was characterized by harmonious order. The earth was at the center of the Ptolemaic universe and the seven planets circled perfectly around the earth, guided by the forces of the crystalline heavens. Unity and proportionality characterized this universe in the same way that creation itself was marked by unity in multiplicity. Bonaventure saw that, within this Ptolemaic universe, everything in creation is ordered one to another, since everything has its proper location, arrangement and purpose. Furthermore, everything is ordered not only *within* creation but is also oriented and directed toward a *telos*, a final goal.[67] Bonaventure perceived such a harmonious connection between the historical and teleological orders that he described them as made to conform to one another.[68] That is, the ordering of things in the universe exists because of the ordering of things toward their final end.

We might find Bonaventure's orderly universe irrelevant today as we continue to discover that we live in an open universe, marked by chaos and complexity. The science of chaos indicates that nonlinear dynamical systems are characterized by spontaneous, emergent changes that give rise to new order within systems. While an open universe means that systems can change over time and form new patterns of behavior, the science of chaos assures us that disorder within the universe is really order in the disguise of disorder. So the bottom line is, order prevails! However, whereas Bonaventure described his orderly universe as teleological, today we are uncertain as to what the *telos* of an evolutionary universe might be. While scientists maintain that we are moving towards an unknown future, theologically we maintain that we are moving towards the promise of God.

Bonaventure's emphasis on the order and harmony of creation impelled him to oppose vehemently the idea of an eternal world. Essentially, the notion of an eternal world means that the world has no beginning and no end. And if there is neither a beginning nor end, matter itself is eternal.[69] Even today, the notion of an eternal world is not favored. Scientists concede that our present universe seems to have had some type of beginning and will have an end, even though it may be billions of years in the future. The eternity of the world, in Bonaventure's view, militated against the order of creation since, without a beginning and end, there could be no true order in creation. For Bonaventure, order requires three terms—a beginning, a middle and an end. Without a beginning, the world would be meaningless because it would have no real relationship with God and, therefore, no God-intended purpose or destiny. Without God as creator, matter itself would be eternal and, if matter is eternal, it can reflect nothing of God. Thus, Bonaventure concluded, the world is not eternal. Rather, it is created by God, in time, out of nothing, by one supreme principle whose power has disposed all things with a certain measure, number and weight.[70] Creation, therefore, has a definite beginning and a definite end. Only in this way does creation have meaning and purpose since only a finite creation can be ordered to an infinite God.

Creation as Dynamic

For Bonaventure, the meaning of creation is summed up in the word "relationship." The basis of creation is the Trinity, a community of relationships out of which creation emerges.[71] All of creation, therefore—rocks, trees, stars, plants, animals and humans—is, in some way, related to the Trinity. Bonaventure, like Francis, did not view the material world as "brute matter," that is, lifeless and inert. Rather, because the material world is created by God, it is like the Trinity itself, dynamic and relational.

Writing in support of the medieval doctrine of hylomorphism (a doctrine he acquired from Alexander of Hales), Bonaventure maintained that all finite beings are composed of matter and form, and are subject to change.[72] The doctrine of hylomorphism was originally developed by the Greek philosopher Aristotle who, contrary to his teacher Plato, maintained that immanent form enters into composition with prime matter. Aristotle's hylomorphism was an attempt to explain how one can accurately predicate the name "substance" of changeable, sensible things. The sensible things of the world are really real, because they are composites of matter and form.[73]

Hylomorphism underscores the fact that everything changes and, if this is true, it means that everything exists in a state of potentiality. The material world, therefore, is not an accumulation of things fixed in time; rather, matter is simply the name that underscores the principle of potentiality. That is, matter is neither spiritual nor corporeal but can be informed by either spiritual or corporeal forms.

Bonaventure not only held to a plurality of forms but he believed, like Augustine, that all forms, except the human soul, were co-created with matter at the beginning of the world and have since resided in matter, and will continue to do so until the end of time.[74] This doctrine of seminal principles imparts a very dynamic view to creation since it is "loaded" with a myriad number of possibilities or active potentialities inserted by God at the beginning of creation. When God creates, God does not bring about new essences but brings to completion or actualization that which is incomplete or potential. In creation, therefore, what is implicit (potential) is made explicit (actualization of potential) by the power, wisdom and goodness of God. By affirming the doctrine of seminal principles, Bonaventure indicates that matter is dynamic and filled with a multiplicity of possibilities (from the beginning of time until the end of time). Everything that will exist until the end of the world already exists potentially within matter.

Freedom in Creation

How God creates is mystery, but Bonaventure maintains that God creates freely. Freedom is inherent to the order of creation. God grants freedom to creation without disrupting the divine intention to which creation is ordered. The fact that the human person emerges in creation, fit for receiving the divine into him/herself is, according to Bonaventure, the unfolding of the Divine Artist's plan. Bonaventure sees the human person as the crown of God's created order.[75] If matter is dynamic and oriented toward form, Bonaventure sees it oriented toward the highest form, the human spirit, open to union with God. He uses the term "spiritual matter" to describe the orientation of matter toward spirit.[76] In his *Commentary on the Second Book of Sentences*, he states that God created matter lacking in final perfection of form so that by reason of its lack of form and its imperfection, matter might cry out for perfection.[77]

That is, God could have created the world as it was intended to be; however, God chose to create it in such a way that it would be perfected only gradually. Herein the notion of freedom plays an important role. For God could have established the world in perfection—in biblical terms—in an entire day rather than over the course of six days. But God's purpose in creating was not simply to establish an order of being. Rather God created in such a way that there would be one in creation (the human person) who would freely choose God and, in choosing God, become like God—perfect in love.[78]

Thus, God created in such a way as to persuade humans, by teaching, moving and delighting them, to seek final perfection.[79] But is God concerned only for humans? Is creation simply to serve humanity? And, if so, is this not the type of anthropocentrism that offends the dignity of creation? Bonaventure states that the material world cries out for perfection but is unable to attain this end on its own. Matter has a drive toward spirit, but only one who is matter and spirit can unite the material world to God.[80] It is for this reason, Bonaventure says, that the human person stands at the center of creation—not to dominate it but to lead it to perfection. It is the human person, he writes, that uniquely reflects the Trinity in the threefold structure of matter, spirit and the union of these.[81] The material world is dependent on human beings to attain their destiny in God. We might say that the spiritual destiny of the material world is bound up with the human journey to God. But in return it is the material world that helps human persons find God. In Bonaventure's view, humanity and creation cannot exist apart from each other and attain true relationship with God. Only in mutual relationship is God's love fully expressed.

The Exemplary World

One of the most important metaphysical questions for Bonaventure concerned the likeness of relationships between God and the created world. The doctrine that defines these relationships is known as "exemplarism."[82] Exemplarism is based on the notion of exemplar or model. Everything that exists is a copy or replica based on a pattern or model. For the Ancient Greeks such as Plato and his followers, such models were not found in this world but were located in a world beyond, a transcendent world. Plato described this ideal world as a world of forms, where the true models of all things that exist can be found. The only way to come to know the truth of things, therefore, is to transcend this world through contemplation.

Bonaventure's doctrine of exemplarism shares similarities with the teaching of Plato. For example, Bonaventure maintained, like

Plato, that the model or archetype of everything that exists resides in a transcendent world. Unlike Plato's world of forms, however, which has nothing in common with the created world, Bonaventure located the world of forms (or archetypes) in the divine Mind, specifically, in the Word of God.[83] The divine Word, as we have said, is the dynamic expression of the Father's goodness. All of the divine ideas of the Father are expressed in the One (divine) Word. Of course, there is really only one idea, and this idea is the infinite content of God's self-knowledge. Thus, divinity not only knows itself and all that it can produce in the created world, but it knows all those things that it will produce as well as those things which are mere possibilities and will never exist. It is for this reason that Bonaventure can say that all possible worlds exist in the Word.[84] In this one Word is everything that ever has existed, that presently exists, that ever will exist or that could ever possibly have existed.

Because the Word of God is the center of the divine ideas, the Word is the model or exemplar of all things. All things are true in relation to the Word. Just as the eternal Word expresses the Father, so too, when the divine ideas of the Word are expressed, creation appears as the art of God. As the Word expresses the Father, creation expresses the Word.[85] This means that everything in creation has its model or exemplar in the Word of God. Thus, when the Word becomes flesh, the center of the Trinity, in whom the truth of all reality exists, appears at the center of creation; thus, the truth of creation is revealed.

Bonaventure described the created universe as the fountain fullness of God's expressed being. As God is expressed in creation, creation, in turn, expresses the Creator. We can compare the manifold variety of things in creation to the stain-glassed windows of a great cathedral. Just as light strikes the various panes of glass and diffracts into an array of colors, so too the divine light emanates through the Word and diffracts in the universe, producing a myriad of "colors" expressed in a myriad of things, all reflecting the divine light in some way.

Creation as Mirror and Book

Bonaventure used two images to describe creation: mirror and book. As a mirror, creation reflects the power, wisdom and goodness of the Trinity precisely by the way things express themselves.[86] However, Bonaventure also describes the created world as a book in which its Maker, the Trinity, shines forth and is represented at three levels of expression: a trace (vestige), an image and a likeness.[87] The difference in these levels of expression reflects the degree of similarity between the creature and Creator, the copy and the model. The trace (or vestige) is the most distant reflection of God and is found in all creatures. That is, every grain of sand, every star, every earthworm reflects the Trinity as its origin (efficient cause), its reason for existence (formal cause) and the end to which it is destined (final cause). Everything that exists, therefore, reflects the power, wisdom and goodness of the Trinity. The image, however, is found only in intellectual (human) beings. It reflects the fact that the human person is not only structured according to the image of the Trinity, but as image, is an apt receptacle for the divine. The human person is structured to express the Trinity in a limited and finite way. Finally, Bonaventure describes those humans conformed to God by grace as likeness (similitude), since, through grace, they bear a likeness to God.

Sacramental Creation

Creation is a theophany for Bonaventure, an expression of God's glory manifested in the sacred order of creation. Because the world expresses the Word through whom all things are made (John 1), every creature is itself a "little word." The universe, therefore, appears as a book representing and describing its Maker. Every creature is an aspect of God's self-expression in the world, and since every creature has its foundation in the Word, each is equally close to God (although the mode of relationship differs). Since the Word of God is expressed in the manifold variety of creation, Bonaventure views the world as sacramental—a symbolic world full of signs of God's presence. The world is created as a means of God's self-revelation so that, like a mirror or footprint, it might lead us to love and praise the Creator. We are created to read the book of creation so that we may know the Author of Life. The world is a sign and is meant to lead humans to what it signifies, namely, the infinite Trinity of dynamic, eternal and self-diffusive love.

The book of creation, according to Bonaventure, was intended by God to be the book of divine wisdom made visible to all; however, this book became unintelligible to humans because of sin.[88] Like a book written in a foreign language, creation became illegible because the human mind, clouded by sin, became enveloped in darkness. When sin rendered this book incomprehensible, Wisdom, the Word, became flesh, so that the book written within (the divine Word) became written without in the humanity of Jesus Christ. In the Incarnation, the divine Word, the ground of all reality, appeared at the center of creation. The Word who is the truth of all things took flesh and was made known in the person of Jesus Christ. One who knows Christ, therefore, knows the truth of reality.

Bonaventure highlights Francis as the exemplary Christ-mystic. Bonaventure perceived the connection between the exemplary world and the centrality of Christ in the life of Francis of Assisi. In his biography of Francis, he describes the exemplary world as it was intended to be. Francis is one who saw divine beauty in the beautiful things of creation because he saw that beauty first in Christ, crucified and glorified upon the cross. Through his relationship with Christ, Francis identified each and every creature as a brother and sister because he recognized that they had the same primordial source (or goodness) as himself. Bonaventure describes this ability to see the reality of things in relation to God as "contuition." Contuition is the consciousness of God's presence together with the object of creation itself whether it be a tree, a flower or a tiny earthworm.[89]

Francis was able to apprehend the real depths of creation because he had entered deeply into the Word incarnate. There, in the center of his being, and now, at the center of creation, he discovered the truth of himself and of all creation in God, namely, that he and creation were "joined at the hip" and were together on the journey to God. Through his relationship with Christ, Francis experienced a transformation of consciousness through grace. His awareness of the created world changed. The created world was no longer an illegible book to him; rather, every aspect of creation spoke to Francis of the love of God revealed in Jesus Christ. Francis was able to read the "words of creation" as the book of God. Everything spoke to him of the love of God manifested in Christ, and he made of all things a ladder to climb up and embrace *"him who is utterly desirable."*[90]

Through the life of Francis we can appreciate the mystery of Jesus Christ as the mystery of the divine Word made flesh by which we come to know the depths of all reality. In a small work called *The Five Feasts of the Child Jesus*, Bonaventure described how Jesus is born within a human soul that is prayerful, humble and dedicated to God. When one finds Jesus within oneself, he indicated, then one may find Jesus in the structures of the created universe.[91] The same idea is expressed theologically throughout his writings. Bonaventure consistently claims that Christ belongs to the very structure of reality—as Word, to the reality of God; as incarnate Word, to the reality of the universe created by God. It is Christ who reveals to the world its own meaning.[92] Since creation is a vast symbol in which God speaks the divine mystery into that which is not divine, creation (especially humans) bears a "congruous" relation to the Word. Because creation is the "expressed word" of the divine Word, it is directed in its inner core to fulfillment and completion in God.

But how shall creation attain its goal? For Bonaventure, the goal is attained through the human person who, like Francis, is conformed to God through grace. Such a person recognizes the divine signs of creation and offers to God praise and thanksgiving. The word "person" is related to the Latin *"per-sonare"* which means "to sound through." To be a person is based not on *what* we do but *who* we are in relation to God and others. It means to be an instrument of otherness by which the other "sounds through" in one's life. In the person of Jesus Christ, God radiated throughout his life, in his words and actions and ultimately in his act of love on the cross.

Francis was also a true person because, like Christ, God's love radiated through him by which he became a brother to all creation. The human person who, like Francis, can offer a conscious loving voice to an otherwise mute creation[93] fills the yearnings of the divine heart—the praise and glory of God chanted by one who can lead creation in a harmony of love. Only the human person has the freedom to bring about peace and reconciliation within creation because only the human person has the capacity to love in union with God. The destiny of creation, therefore, depends on how we love.

PART FOUR
JOHN DUNS SCOTUS'S
THEOLOGY OF CREATION

While Bonaventure described an intimate link between the Trinity and creation, a link that affirms the goodness of creation, the fourteenth-century theologian, John Duns Scotus, viewed the goodness of creation through the lens of the primacy of Christ, the freedom of God, and the contingency of the world. Scotus's doctrine of creation is insightful and original. It imparts to creation a profound dignity that reflects Francis's fidelity to the world as the cloister in which we seek God.

Creation: Gift of God's Infinite Love

Scotus looked at our world and realized that God is absolutely free; nothing created is necessary. Since God did not have to create anything, all is gift and grace.[94] God creates in order to reveal and communicate God's self to others as the fullness of divine love. God reveals this love by choosing to create this world precisely as it is. The present moment, therefore, expresses the perfection of the eternal. For Scotus, *why* creation comes about is more important than *how* creation comes about. Scotus claims that God creates for God's own purpose, namely, the glory and love of God. Creation is simply the work of an infinitely loving Creator.

Scotus, like Francis and Bonaventure, saw an intimate connection between creation and Incarnation, a connection that he grounded in the infinite love of God. The reason for all divine activity, he said, is found in the very nature of God as love. God is Trinity and Trinity, for Scotus, is the three divine persons in a communion of love. As the eternal movement of lover (Father), beloved (Son) and the sharing of love (Spirit), the Trinity is the model of reality, especially for human relationships. According to Scotus, God's love is ordered, free and holy. Every single aspect of the created universe exists because of God's absolute freedom and because of God's unlimited love. All of creation is a gift. Nothing in creation is necessary.[95] God loves God's very self in the other, and this love is unselfish since God is the cause of all creatures. Divine love tends to "spill over" or diffuse itself, and God wills to be loved by another who can love God as perfectly as God does. This "other" of God's infinite love is Jesus Christ.

Scotus maintains that God became human in Jesus out of love (rather than because of human sin) because God wanted to express God's self in a creature who would be a masterpiece and who would love God perfectly in return. This is Scotus's doctrine of the primacy of Christ. Christ is the first in God's intention to love. Creation is not an independent act of divine love that was, incidentally, followed up by divine self-revelation in the covenant. Rather, the divine desire to become incarnate was part of the overall plan or order of intention. Scotus places the Incarnation within the context of creation and not within the context of human sin. Christ, therefore, is the masterpiece of love, the "*summum opus Dei.*" The idea that *all* of creation is made for Christ means that for Christ to come about there had to be a creation, and, in this creation, there had to be beings capable of understanding and freely responding to divine initiative. Creation was only a prelude to a much fuller manifestation of divine goodness, namely, the Incarnation.[96]

Christ: The Blueprint of Creation

Whereas Thomas Aquinas emphasized the material and formal causes in creation, Scotus emphasized the final cause as determining the work of the Artist. Everything in creation is related to finality expressed in Christ, and this final goal is impressed on everything in between. Christ is the meaning and model of creation and every creature is made in the image of Christ. Because creation is centered on Incarnation, every leaf, cloud, fruit, animal and person is an outward expression of the Word of God in love. When Jesus comes as the Incarnation of God, there is a "perfect fit" because everything has been made to resemble Jesus Christ.[97] This means that sun, moon, trees, animals, stories, all have life only in Christ, through Christ and with Christ, for Christ is the Word through whom all things are made (cf. John 1:1).[98]

The idea that all of creation is "christoform" finds a parallel in Bonaventure's *Sermon on the Resurrection,* where he writes that in his transfiguration Christ shares existence with all things: with the stones, he shares existence; with plants he shares life; with animals he shares sensation; and with angels he shares intelligence. "In his human nature," Bonaventure writes, "Christ embraces something of every creature in himself."[99] Bonaventure, therefore, sees the whole of creation related to the mystery of Christ. Christ is not an abstract concept. Rather, Christ is the Word incarnate, crucified and glorified, and the fullness of this incarnate Word embraces the whole of creation.

Scotus, too, maintained that Christ is the blueprint for creation. As the *motif* or pattern of creation, Christ is the perfect divine-human communion who exemplifies the meaning and purpose of all creation, namely, the praise and glory of God in a communion of love. All of creation is to be transformed into a communion of love centered in Christ. Scotus's christocentric vision finds something of its expression in Francis's *Canticle of the Creatures,* in which Francis sings of his fraternal relationships with all the elements of creation. This cosmic hymn, with Christ as its center, is a hymn of the Trinity in which the universe, bound together in and through the cosmic Christ, offers praise and glory to God.

Univocity of Being

The question of how we know God in and through the created world takes on a deeper meaning through Scotus's notion of univocity of being.[100] This concept refers to the way God's being and created being are related through the one concept of "being." For some theologians, like Thomas Aquinas, created reality participates in God's being without ever attaining unity with God's being. That is, God's being and created being are two separate orders of being. Thus, created being can only indicate to us what God's being is *like* (analogy of being), not what God's being *is.* For Scotus, however, univocal being has a distinctive and exclusive transcendentality as being and also as one, true and good (although Scotus did not call univocal being "God" but rather "first principle"). He described the relationship of (all) beings to the one, true and good in terms that stress their unity.[101] God, therefore, does not exist outside the relational ordering of being, as if only the effects were ordered and the cause lay outside the relationship. That is, the first principle (God) does not transcend order. Rather, creation is related to God and God is related to creation. The essential order represents the unified whole of all that is, including God.

For Scotus, God's being and created being are not identical. Nevertheless, the concept "being" (*ens*) stands as the foundation between the mind and reality and is the way we come to know and understand the world around us, ourselves and God. God's being and created being are two distinct *modes* of being: infinite and finite. Uncreated, necessary being is infinite. Created, contingent beings are finite. The best way to understand this central and univocal concept is by asking: what is there? As we face reality, we are aware of the presence of something or someone. This act of presence to us gives rise to the question, who is it? what is it? It is an act by which the mind turns its attention and presence to the world. The univocity of being and essential ordering, therefore, offers a simple explanation for the relationship between knowing and being. Because of this relationship we are able to understand something of the world in which we live. Everything makes a piece of a unified whole that reveals the rationality, freedom and creativity of God.[102]

On a more mundane level, the univocity of being means that each created thing, in its own way, tells us something about God. Things do not express simply an aspect of God, but rather each and every thing reveals God's beauty as a whole. The notion of the univocity of being therefore imparts to the things of creation a tremendous dignity, as well as a sense of mystery and awe. Because God's being is the foundation of the natural order, the ineffable is made effable through the concrete existence of all reality. The divine is mystery that can be apprehended by reason, although the fullness of the mystery lies beyond reason. Whereas Bonaventure claims that creation is like a mirror reflecting the divine or like a stained-glass window through which the divine light shines, Scotus maintains that the created order is endowed with its own light that shines from within. Creation is not a window but a lamp, and each unique created being radiates the light of God.

The Unique Love of God and the Doctrine of *Haecceitas*

This idea that the divine mystery can be experienced within the created order of being relates to Scotus's doctrine of the primacy of

Christ. The move from the metaphysical relationship of the essential order to the revealed relationship of covenant and Incarnation is contained within a single, intentional divine act of love, namely, the Incarnation. This ordering of all things towards Christ is clear in Francis's Admonition V: "Consider, O human being, in what great excellence the Lord God has placed you, for He created you and formed you *to the image* of His beloved Son according to the body, and to *His likeness* according to the Spirit."[103] Francis seems to have intuited that before humans were created Christ was intended, for we are made in the image of Christ. Christ is the pattern, therefore, the intentional blueprint for the created. The Incarnation sets the stage for all that God does. The humanity of Jesus, we might say, is the point of God's creating everything.

This attentiveness to the details of nature as the revelation of God is faithful to the original intuition of Francis and his attention to the smallest creatures as sacraments of God. Scotus, however, develops this insight in a more concrete way as the experience of God. His notion of individuation points to the idea that each particular being has its own intrinsic, unique and proper being. Scotus placed great emphasis on the inherent dignity of each and every thing that exists. We often perceive individual things through their accidental individual characteristics (e.g., size, shape, color), but Scotus calls our attention to the very "thisness" of each thing, the very being of the object that makes it itself and not something else (a "not-that"). Scotus's notion of essential "thisness" is known as the doctrine of *haecceitas* and relates to essential individuation.[104] For Scotus, individuation must be based in the very substance of a thing or person, not in some accidental aspect of a thing or person. The notion of *haecceitas* points to individuality at the core of each thing— its very being.[105] It refers to the positive dimension of every concrete and contingent being that identifies it and makes it worthy of attention. *Haecceitas* makes a singular what it is and sets it off from other things like it to which it might be compared. It can only be known by direct acquaintance, not from any consideration of common nature.

The notion of *haecceitas* in view of the primacy of Christ signifies that Jesus is the model on which God models every aspect of creation: sun, stars, snails, raindrops, oxygen, magnesium protons, grapes. In this respect, the smallest things of creation, for example, a leaf or a grain of sand, become charged with divine meaning. Each does something, and what it does is "itself." This "do-being" is doing Christ.[106] Such a view of nature leads to a poetry in which things are not specific symbols, but all mean one and the same thing—the beauty of Christ in whom they are created.[107]

Scotus's doctrine had a strong influence on the Jesuit poet Gerard Manley Hopkins, whose attention to the "inscape" of nature reflected Scotus's view of creation. For Hopkins, following Scotus, the smallest things of creation, for example, a leaf or a grain of sand, is not just a symbol of Christ. If it simply reminded us of something about Christ, for example, his humility or meekness, it would have no real value of its own. Instead, we would simply abstract a quality from the grain of sand or leaf and use it to describe Christ. The quality of a thing would be associated with the quality of a person. But the sand-grain or leaf itself would not be all that important; a small acorn or tomato could do the job as well. They are dispensable, interchangeable. They are used to achieve some other purpose, to teach a lesson, usually a moral one. This is a view of nature in which true being exists only in God, and all other being is derivative, pointing toward true being, but only weakly and indirectly. What Hopkins grasped through Scotus is that the sand-grain, by being/doing itself, directly and immediately *does* God, who is incarnate, Christ. That is, the sand-grain does *all* of Christ, not just this or that aspect of him.[108] Hopkins describes this insight in one of his poems:

> As kingfishers catch fire, dragonflies draw flame; . . .
> Deals out that being indoors each one dwells;
> Selves—goes itself; *myself* it speaks and spells,
> Crying *What I do is me: for that I came.*
>
> I say more: the just man justices;
> Keeps grace: that keeps all his goings graces;
> Acts in God's eye what in God's eye he is—
> Christ—for Christ plays in ten thousand places,
> Lovely in limbs, and lovely in eyes not his
> To the Father through the features of men's faces.[109]

Scotus's theology of creation is one in which grace and nature intertwine. Nothing in creation is accidental or excessive; nothing is worthless or trivial. Each and every thing, no matter how small or seemingly insignificant, is of infinite value because it images God in its own unique being. Scotus's doctrine, therefore, not only highlights the individual significance of created things, but it provides ample room for diversity in creation. Indeed, the more diverse the creation, the greater the glory of God. We humans are called to observe closely, attentively and carefully that things are and do themselves. And it is in doing/being themselves that they are Christ.[110]

In short, things are God-like in their specificity. Thus, regular, daily attention to the wider world of creatures/nature is fundamental. The importance of vision here is the same as we find in Francis and Bonaventure. "The world is charged with the grandeur of God,"[111] and we are called to see deeply into the reality of things just as a scientist probes the structure of the living cell through a microscope. Without such attention we begin to lose living contact with Christ in his most widely extended body, the universe.

A Christ-Centered Universe

It is not surprising that the Jesuit paleontologist Pierre Teilhard de Chardin was attracted to Scotus's doctrine. When he discovered Scotus's teaching through the Sicilian Franciscan, Father Allegra, he claimed "Voila! La théologie de l'avenir!" (There! The future of theology!) Teilhard, like Scotus, perceived Christ not only at the heart of the universe but at the heart of the material universe. In *The Divine Milieu*, Teilhard remarks: "[Through the Incarnation] there is nothing here that is profane for those who know how to see."[112] By this he meant that Christ, physically and literally, fills the universe. Christ is immersed in space and in the unfolding of time in our human existence. Teilhard, like Scotus, saw an intrinsic relationship between Christ and the physical universe—Christ belongs to the very structure of the cosmos.

We may also point out that Teilhard, like Scotus, saw Christian action as that which shapes a Christic universe.[113] Our lives in union with Christ must help sacramentalize the universe. For Scotus, the beauty of the present moment expresses the perfection of the eternal; however, beauty is revealed when we humans strive to make the right choices that correspond to a God who is infinite love. Since all of reality is good and beautiful, moral loving does not so much involve finding those objects worthy of love (since all reality is good) but rather working out the manner by which we can love reality as it deserves.[114]

My moral loving involves my relationship to all beings that surround me and my efforts to strengthen and enhance their mutuality. Like Francis, Scotus maintains that relationship is the key to the beauty of the universe. Since all reality is good, my relationships with others, human and non-human, ought to promote goodness.[115] This is what justice is for Scotus—the orientation of rational beings towards right loving and right action. Justice is a stance toward reality. It involves treating everything in creation as it deserves. It calls us to attend to the "thisness," the inherent dignity, of each and every thing that exists. When we act justly and love rightly, when we treat things with utmost dignity according to their inherent goodness, realizing that each unique thing is singularly wanted and loved by God, then we help promote the harmony of goodness. This is the harmony of a diverse and created order in which the whole of creation gives glory and praise to God, the infinitely loving Creator.

PART FIVE
SUMMARY

Viewing the doctrine of creation through the writings of Francis, Bonaventure and Scotus, we can identify themes that form a continuous thread of ideas: 1) the goodness of creation, 2) the integral relationship between Christ and creation, 3) the sacramentality of creation, 4) the integral relationship between the human and the non-human aspects of creation, and 5) the universe as a divine milieu with Christ as center.

First, the goodness of creation. From the life of Francis we affirm the overflowing goodness of the triune God as the source of creation. Creation flows out of the heart of an infinitely loving Creator. The Franciscan tradition emphasizes that creation is made for Christ and not Christ for creation. It is Christ who opens our eyes to the goodness of creation in such a way that a Franciscan theology of creation without Christ is incomplete.

Second, the integral relationship between Christ and creation. Because of the intimate relationship between Christ and creation, we may say that Francis's own approach to creation was mystical. As his life became immersed in Christ's, he found himself immersed in creation, related to the things of creation in the same way he was related to Christ—as a brother of compassionate love. Francis's grasp of his integral relationship to creation took a lifetime of conversion in the same way that the things of nature require time to grow to maturity. Through greater attention to the details of nature, he came to realize that everything bears enormous dignity because of its relationship to Christ, and he related to each and every thing as singularly loved by God. He perceived the overflowing goodness of God in the beautiful things of creation, and he realized that this goodness, the source of his own life, is the same source of everything that exists. Through poverty, humility and compassionate love, Francis came to dwell in the world as in a cloister, for he came to realize that the world is the cloister of God.

Third, the sacramentality of creation. The notion of the sacramentality of creation was taken up by Bonaventure and given a deeper theological meaning. Bonaventure drew an integral relation between the Trinity of self-diffusive goodness and the goodness of creation. The whole of creation emerging out of the fecundity of divine goodness reflects an intimate relationship to the Creator and is oriented to God as its source and goal.

Fourth, the integral relationship between the human and the non-human aspects of creation. The relationship between the human and the non-human aspects of creation acquires a rich theological meaning in the writings of Bonaventure and Scotus. Both concede that the richness of the divine mystery of love provides a basis for explaining the richness and diversity of the created world. God is the mystery of self-diffusive love that is beyond measure. If the world is, in some way, an external expression of that mystery, and if no single created word can give adequate expression to the richness of that mystery, it is not surprising that there is a rich variety in creation through which the eternal mystery of love finds expression. Bonaventure conceived of God in terms of divine simplicity and boundless fertility. He viewed creation in similar terms. At one level, the elements of the created order are few and simple. But they come together to produce the richness of both non-living and living forms. It is no wonder that for Bonaventure the created order is a rich symbol that mediates to us the simplicity and richness of the divine mystery.[116]

Bonaventure's view of creation as a book and mirror reflecting God was given new and profound meaning in the writings of Scotus. It is Scotus who affirms that creation is good precisely in the diversity of everything that exists. God willed creation just as it ought to be. Scotus drew an intimate link between creation and Incarnation and clearly maintained that the universe is made for Christ. In Scotus's view, it is the primacy of Christ that imparts an inherent dignity to everything that exists in creation, and he develops this idea through his doctrine of individuation or *haecceitas*. That is, everything in its unique being, its "thisness," is related to Christ, who is the blueprint of the universe.

Fifth, the universe as a divine milieu with Christ as center. While the centrality of Christ in creation is fundamental to Franciscan theology, the primacy of Christ is not unique to Scotus. Rather, both Bonaventure and Scotus maintain that creation is moving towards the fullness of Christ. Bonaventure's notion of spiritualized matter, whereby matter tends toward spirit, corresponds to Teilhard de Chardin's notion of Christogenesis. Bonaventure identifies Christ as the "noble perfection" of the universe,[117] whereas Teilhard speaks of Christ as the Omega Point, the one toward whom the whole evolutionary universe is progressing. Like Teilhard, the Franciscan theologians maintain that a universe without Christ is incomplete, since Christ is the head and center of the universe and the one toward whom the universe is oriented. Incarnation is what creation is about. For Scotus (as for Bonaventure), the notion of Incarnation involves the whole created order whereby Christ is the purpose and goal of the universe. In this respect, Scotus's doctrine is reflected in the cosmic Incarnation of Francis's *Canticle of the Creatures* whereby everything is related to every other thing because everything is related to Christ who is "Brother Sun," the radiance of the Most High. Just as Francis saw nothing trivial in creation, so too Scotus maintained that everything is to manifest the glory of God.

The fundamental relationship between Incarnation and creation leads to the central idea that each and every aspect of creation has absolute dignity because everything is created specifically and uniquely through the Word of God. We humans are related to the non-human things of creation because we are congruently related to the Word of God. God's love is the basis of everything that exists, and creation is the cloister where we encounter the God of compassionate love. The unity of love, however, depends on the human person who is created to love in a unique and personal way. The way we love depends on how we use the gift of freedom. It is in the diversity of creation, bound in a unity of love, that God's glory is manifested. Christ is the center of the universe and the one through whom our passage into God takes place. When we humans realize that all of creation is on the journey to God, then will the universe attain peace and unity in love. Then will it become the fullness of Christ in whom God will be all in all.

CONCLUSION:
WHAT IS OURS TO DO?

Standing on such a deep and powerful tradition, how should Franciscans today relate to creation? How can we understand the human journey to God as one that includes creation? How can the tradition help us overcome violence to creation and restore relationships of peace and justice? Is it enough simply to "recycle" or "turn off the lights" or does our tradition call us to a more radical stance with regard to creation? Here are some points to consider:

- We must realize our interconnectedness to creation. Part of our poverty is to realize our dependency on the things of the created world. The Franciscan tradition, left to us by Francis, offers the familial model of relating to creation. Franciscan spirituality means changing our internal focus or consciousness. A new consciousness must call us to an active stance as "brother" and "sister" to the non-human creation.

- Developing a new Franciscan consciousness also means an awareness of the intrinsic value of everything that exists. We need to pay attention to the details of creation and strive to gaze contemplatively on nature. Such gazing into things is a way of seeing Christ.

- Following the Franciscan emphasis on a Christ-centered universe, contact with nature needs to be a fundamental component of our Franciscan way of life. A trip to the ocean, a walk in the woods, working in the garden, etc. are important, not primarily for what they produce, but for their inherent Christ-contact. As Hopkins wrote to a friend: "I think that the trivialness of life is, and personally to each one ought to be seen to be, done away with by the Incarnation."[118]

- We must come to realize that our sinful actions are at the root of our present ecological crisis and thus our need for ongoing penance or conversion. The Franciscan practice of penance embodies humility. It consists in acknowledging our brokenness and sinfulness. The practice of "eco-penance" is both an interior attitude and a praxis. It can promote consistency between the statement of values we make about creation and our behavior toward it.

- Believing in the inherent goodness of creation and the dignity of each created thing should lead to a stance on environmental justice. Justice entails right and loving relationships and thus a stance to oppose or change relationships that exploit the poor or cause environmental hazards to the poor.

- Awareness of biological diversity as an expression of the goodness of God means addressing the interdependence of the many forms of life on our planet. It is realizing that injury or extinction of one species can affect an entire ecosystem. It is having a greater awareness that we and the universe are "joined at the hip."

- Finally, it is helpful to realize that we live in an evolutionary universe with Christ as the center and goal. To be Franciscans in an evolutionary universe is to have an awareness that our actions can help move the universe towards its fulfillment in Christ, or they may thwart this goal. What we do matters to the matter of the universe. The world will not be destroyed. It will be brought to the conclusion that God intends for it from the beginning. And that beginning is intertwined with the mystery of the incarnate Word and the glorified Christ. With Christ, all the lines of energy in the universe are coordinated and unified; all comes together in unity and coherence; and all is finally brought to its destiny with God.[119]

How shall we come to stand in the midst of creation as poor mendicants? The life of Francis shows us that only Christ can lead us to the truth of who we are in relation to God, the truth that all creation is on a journey to God. As pilgrims and strangers in the world we are called to be in solidarity with every aspect of creation, realizing that creation is incomplete and yearns for its completion in God. As Franciscans in the twenty-first century, we are heirs to a rich theological tradition that can provide a framework for incorporating environmental sensitivity into religious practice and activity.

We are a resource for the Church, and we are capable of embodying Francis's passionate love of creation in our word and in our example.[120]

DISCUSSION QUESTIONS

1. What are we doing at present to nurture our familial relationship with the environment?

2. Is creation integral or secondary to our relationship with God? Do we view our relationship to creation as part of our journey into God?

3. What type of environmental "habits" must we adopt as Franciscans to promote justice for the earth?

4. How do we understand the relationship between Incarnation and creation?

5. What aspects of Francis's spirituality can help us become more "ecologically sensitive?"

NOTES

[1]Ian G. Barbour, *Religion and Science: Historical and Contemporary Issues* (New York: HarperCollins, 1997), 195.

[2]Lynn White, Jr. "The Historical Roots of Our Ecological Crisis," *Science* 155 (March 10, 1967): 1205. I begin with this influential essay, but it is important to note that White's essay and his interpretation of the Christian tradition has been well critiqued by historians.

[3]White, 1207.

[4]White, 1206.

[5]White, 1206-07.

[6]It is worth noting that biblical scholars generally reject White's analysis of the Genesis text. See, among others, Bernhard Anderson, "'Subdue the Earth': What Does It Mean?" *Bible Review* 8/5 (Oct. 1992): 4, 10; Richard Clifford, "Genesis 1-3: Permission to Exploit Nature?" *The Bible Today* 20 (1988): 133-7; James Barr, "Man and Nature—The Ecological Controversy and the Old Testament," *Bulletin of the John Rylands Library* 55 (1972-73): 9-32; Gene Tucker, "Creation and the Limits of the World: Nature and History in the Old Testament," *Horizons in Biblical Theology* 15 (1993): 105-18.

[7]Roger D. Sorrell, *St. Francis of Assisi and Nature: Tradition and Innovation in Western Christian Attitudes toward the Environment* (New York: Oxford University Press, 1988), 7.

[8]Eric Doyle, *St. Francis and the Song of Brotherhood* (New York: Seabury Press, 1981), 41.

[9]Doyle, 42.

[10]Sean Edward Kinsella, "How Great a Gladness: Some Thoughts on Francis of Assisi and the Natural World," *Studies in Spirituality* 12 (2002): 66. According to Plato's Allegory of the Cave, which was very influential on the structure of Neoplatonism, sensible reality is comprised of ersatz forms while the true forms lie in a transcendent, spiritual world.

[11]Kinsella, 90; Cf. also, Ewert Cousins, "Francis of Assisi: Christian Mysticism at the Crossroads," in *Mysticism and Religious Traditions*, ed. S. Katz (New York: Oxford, 1983), 164-5.

[12]Sorrell, *St. Francis of Assisi*, 89; Cousins, "Francis of Assisi," 165.

[13]Paul M. Allen and Joan deRis Allen, *Francis of Assisi's Canticle of the Creatures: A Modern Spiritual Path* (New York: Continuum, 1996), 45.

[14]Ewert Cousins, "Francis of Assisi and Bonaventure: Mysticism and Theological Interpretation," in *The Other Side of God*, ed. Peter L. Berger (New York: Anchor Press, 1981), 80.

[15]*Heresy and Authority in Medieval Europe*, ed. Edward Peters (Philadelphia: University of Pennsylvania Press, 1980), 104.

[16]Raoul Manselli, *St. Francis of Assisi*, trans. Paul Duggan (Chicago: Franciscan Herald Press, 1988), 4-5.

[17]Murray Bodo, *The Threefold Way of Saint Francis* (New York: Paulist, 2000), 21; Manselli, *St. Francis*, 5; Edward Peters, ed., *Heresy and Authority in Medieval Europe* (Philadelphia: University of Pennsylvania Press, 1980), 103-37.

[18]Peters, *Heresy and Authority*, 123.

[19]Manselli, *St. Francis*, 5.

[20]Francis of Assisi, *Testament* 3, in *Francis of Assisi: Early Documents*, vol. 1, *The Saint*, ed. Regis J. Armstrong, J. A. Wayne Hellmann, and William J. Short (New York: New City Press, 1999), 124. Hereafter this volume will be referred to as *FA:ED* 1 followed by page numbers.

[21]Thomas of Celano, *The Remembrance of the Desire of a Soul*, in *Francis of Assisi: Early Documents*, vol. 2, *The Founder*, ed. Regis J. Armstrong, J. A. Wayne Hellmann, and William J.

Ilia Delio, O.S.F.

Short (New York: New City Press, 2000), 249. Hereafter this volume will be referred to as *FA:ED* 2 followed by page numbers.

[22]Bonaventure, *The Major Legend of Saint Francis*, in FA:ED 2, 533.

[23]See *Angela of Foligno: Complete Works*, trans. Paul Lachance (New York: Paulist, 1993), 169-70.

[24]Thomas of Celano, *The Life of Saint Francis*, in *FA:ED* 1, 185.

[25]It is worth noting that the biographies of Celano and Bonaventure were composed for the benefit of the Franciscan Order and thus incorporate theological interpretations that helped shape Francis's vernacular theology into more acceptable theological forms. Bonaventure, for example, was part of the Christian Neoplatonic tradition and tried to integrate Francis's experience into the mainstream, speculative Neoplatonic tradition, as in his *Soul's Journey Into God*. Yet, as Ewert Cousins points out, Bonaventure not only drew the innovations of Francis's experience into the established tradition, but at the same time he transformed the tradition by these innovations. On the one hand, Bonaventure's speculative Neoplatonism was in sharp contrast with the prophetic visionary mysticism of Francis, while, on the other hand, he assimilated Francis's innovative Christ-centered religious experience into the Christian Neoplatonic tradition. As a result, Cousins claims, Bonaventure "Franciscanized" Neoplatonism. See Ewert Cousins, "Francis of Assisi: Christian Mysticism at the Crossroads," 169, 176, 187.

[26]Doyle, *Song of Brotherhood*, 6.

[27]Doyle, *Song of Brotherhood*, 32.

[28]Doyle, *Song of Brotherhood*, 32-3.

[29]Doyle, *Song of Brotherhood*, 41.

[30]The word *pietas* is defined as an attitude of respect toward those to whom one is bound by ties of religion, consanguinity; of relationships between human beings: a. of children to parents, b. of parents to children; c. between husband and wife, d. of other relationships. See *Oxford Latin Dictionary*, ed. P. G. W. Glare (Oxford: Clarendon Press, 1982, repr. 1983), 1378.

[31]Bonaventure, *The Major Legend*, in FA:ED 2, 531.

[32]Bonaventure, *Major Legend*, in FA:ED 2, 591.

[33]Bonaventure, *Major Legend*, in FA:ED 2, 584-5.

[34]Celano, *Remembrance of the Desire of a Soul*, in FA:ED 2, 354.

[35]Celano, *Remembrance of the Desire of a Soul*, in FA:ED 2, 354-55.

[36]Celano, *Life of Francis*, in FA:ED 1, 250-51.

[37]Timothy Vining, "A Theology of Creation Based on the Life of Francis of Assisi," *The Cord* 40 (1990): 105.

[38]Bonaventure, *Major Legend*, in FA:ED 2, 590.

[39]Celano, *Life of Francis*, in FA:ED 1, 255.

[40]Bonaventure, *The Major Legend*, in FA:ED 2, 551.

[41]Bonaventure, *The Major Legend*, in FA:ED 2, 596-7.

[42]Bonaventure, *The Major Legend*, in FA:ED 2, 586.

[43]Celano, *The Remembrance of the Desire of a Soul*, in FA:ED 2, 358.

[44]Bonaventure, *The Major Legend*, in FA:ED 2, 590-595. Cf. also Jean Daniélou, *Sacramentum Futuri: Etudes sur les origines de la typologie biblique* (Paris: J. Vrin, 1950), who states that such animal stories signify the restoration of paradise made possible by Christ to those who believe in him. It is an anticipation of the messianic fulfillment at the end of the ages where there will be a new heaven and a new earth.

[45]Celano, *The Remembrance of the Desire of a Soul*, in FA:ED 2, 357.

[46]Bonaventure, *The Major Legend*, in FA:ED 2, 596.

A Franciscan View of Creation

[47]Celano, *Life of Francis*, in *FA:ED* 1, 257.

[48]Although there is no specific mention of Jesus Christ in this hymn, the brother-sister relationships that Francis describes echo his sense of family relationships in his *Later Version of the Letter to the Faithful*, where he writes: "We are spouses when the faithful soul is joined to Jesus Christ by the Holy Spirit. We are brothers when we do the will of his Father who is in heaven. We are mothers when we carry Him in our heart and body through love and a pure and sincere conscience; we give birth to Him through His holy manner of working, which should shine before others as an example. See FA:ED 1, 49. Familial relationships for Francis are grounded in the Trinity (Father-Son-Spirit) and the integral relationship between the Trinity and Christ. A Trinitarian theology with Christ as center seems to underlie the *Canticle of the Creatures*.

[49]Susanna Peters Coy, "The Problem of 'Per' in the *Cantico di frate sole* of Saint Francis," *Modern Language Notes* 91 (1976): 1-11.

[50]Francis of Assisi, *The Canticle of Creatures*, in *FA:ED* 1, 113-14.

[51]Eloi Leclerc, *The Canticle of Creatures: Symbols of Union*, trans. Matthew J. O'Connell (Chicago: Franciscan Herald Press, 1970), 222.

[52]Leonard Lehmann, *Tiefe und Weite: Der universale Grundzug in den Gebeten des Franziskus von Assisi* (Werl: Dietrick-Coelde-Verlag, 1984), 312.

[53]Kenan B. Osborne, *The Franciscan Intellectual Tradition: Tracing its Origins and Identifying its Central Components*, Vol. 1, The Franciscan Heritage Series (CFIT/ESC-OFM) (St. Bonaventure, NY: Franciscan Institute Publications, 2003), 38.

[54]Ilia Delio, "The *Canticle of Brother Sun*: A Song of Christ Mysticism," *Franciscan Studies* 52 (1992): 20.

[55]Ewert Cousins, *Bonaventure and the Coincidence of Opposites* (Chicago: Franciscan Herald Press, 1978), 29-30.

[56]Zachary Hayes, *Bonaventure: Mystical Writings* (New York: Crossroad, 1999), 15.

[57]Bonaventure, *The Soul's Journey into God, 5:8,* in *Bonaventure: The Soul's Journey into God, The Tree of Life, The Life of St. Francis,* trans. Ewert Cousins (New York: Paulist Press, 1978), 100.

[58]Bernard McGinn first introduced the concept of vernacular theology in *Meister Eckhart and the Beguine Mystics* (New York: Continuum, 1994), 4-14 and further developed it in *The Flowering of Mysticism*, vol. 3, *The Presence of God: A History of Western Mysticism* (New York: Crossroads, 1998), 18-24. Jean Leclercq summarizes the relation between monastic and scholastic theology in "The Renewal of Theology," *Renaissance and Renewal in the Twelfth Century*, ed. Robert Benson and Giles Constable (Cambridge: Harvard University Press, 1982), 68-87.

[59]I *Sent.* prooem. (I, 1-6). The critical edition of Bonaventure's works is the *Opera Omnia* ed. PP. Collegii S. Bonaventurae, 10 vols. (Quaracchi, 1882-1902). Latin texts are indicated by volume and page number in parentheses.

[60]Alexander Gerken, *La théologie du verbe: La relation entre l'Incarnation et la Création selon S. Bonaventure*, trans. Jacqueline Greal (Paris: Éditions Franciscaines, 1970), 132; Zachary Hayes, "Incarnation and Creation in St. Bonaventure," in *Studies Honoring Ignatius Brady, Friar Minor,* ed. Romano Stephen Almagno and Conrad L. Harkins (St. Bonaventure, NY: The Franciscan Institute, 1976), 314.

[61]*Hex.* 12.3 (V, 385).

[62]See I *Sent.* d. 44, q. 1, a. 3, concl. (I, 786a). "Optime ordinatae sunt res in finem, salvo ordine universi, quia universum est tamquam pulcherrimum carmen, quod decurrit secundum optimas consonantias."

[63]II *Sent.* d. 1, p. 2., a. 2., q. 1., concl. (II, 44b). Bonaventure frequently cited Proverbs 16:4.

[64]Zachary Hayes, "Bonaventure: Mystery of the Triune God," in *The History of Franciscan Theology,* ed. Kenan Osborne (St. Bonaventure, NY: The Franciscan Institute, 1994), 64.

[65]See Cousins (trans.) *The Soul's Journey into God,* 1:14-15 in *Bonaventure,* 65-68.

Ilia Delio, O.S.F.

[66]Bonaventure, *Commentarius in librum Ecclesiastes* 1.7 (V, 13b); Bonaventure, *Breviloquium* (*Brev.*) 2.11.2. Engl. trans. José de Vinck, *Breviloquium*, vol. 2, *Works of Bonaventure* (Paterson, NJ: St. Anthony Guild Press, 1963), 101.
[67]*I Sent.* d. 47, a. u. 3, concl. (I, 844a-b). Bonaventure writes: "Duplex enim est ordo rerum: unus in universo, alter in finem."
[68]*II Sent. d.* 15, a. 2, q. 3 (II, 387); *Hex.* 3.6 (V, 344).
[69]Efrem Bettoni, *Saint Bonaventure*, trans. Angelus Gambatese (Notre Dame: University of Notre Dame Press, 1964), 57-9.
[70]*Brev.* 2.1 (V, 219).
[71]Alexander Schaeffer, "The Position and Function of Man in the Created World According to Bonaventure," *Franciscan Studies* 20 (1960): 266-67; Leonard Bowman, "The Cosmic Exemplarism of Bonaventure," *Journal of Religion* 55 (1975): 183.
[72]Hayes, "Bonaventure: Mystery of the Triune God," 69-70; Bettoni, *Bonaventure*, 73.
[73]Christopher M. Cullen, "The Semiotic Metaphysics of Saint Bonaventure," Ph. D. dissertation (Washington, DC: Catholic University of America, 1999), 254.
[74]Hayes, "Bonaventure: Mystery of the Triune God," 72-9. For a discussion on Bonaventure's view of matter and form, see Kent Emery, "Reading the World Rightly and Squarely: Bonaventure's Doctrine of the Cardinal Virtues," *Traditio* 39 (1983): 188-99.
[75]*Brev.* 2.4 (V, 222).
[76]*II Sent.* d. 17, a. 1, q. 2, resp. (II, 414-415).
[77]*II Sent.* d. 12, a. 1, q. 3 concl. (II, 298); Emery, "Reading the World Rightly," 195. Bonaventure further indicates that God chose to effect this gradual perfection (of matter) over a course of six days because six, the sum and multiple of its integers, is the perfect number.
[78]Hayes states: "Man is creation that has become aware of itself in knowledge and freedom." See Hayes, "Incarnation and Creation," 318.
[79]*II Sent.* d. 15, a. 2, q. 1, concl. (II, 383).
[80]Bonaventure, *De reductione artium ad theologiam* (*Red. art.*) 20 (V, 324b). English translation, Sister Emma Thérèse Healy, *Saint Bonaventure's De Reductione Artium ad Theologiam*, in *Works of Saint Bonaventure*, vol. I, (St. Bonaventure, NY: The Franciscan Institute, 1955).
[81]Schaeffer, "Position and Function of Man," 295.
[82]Exemplarism is defined as the doctrine of the relations of expression between God and creatures. See J. M. Bissen, *L'Exemplarisme Divin selon saint Bonaventure* (Paris: J. Vrin, 1929), 4; Bowman, "Cosmic Exemplarism," 183-98.
[83]*I Sent.* d. 35, a. u., q. 2 (I, 605); *Hex.* 1.13 (V, 331); *Hex.* 3.4 (V, 343).
[84]*III Sent.* d. 1, a. 2, q. 2, ad 2 (III, 26). The possibility of many world orders is related to the fruitfulness of God's goodness, which ultimately must be traced back to the fecundity of the Father who communicates goodness to the Word. Thus, the possibility of many world orders is expressed in the Word.
[85]Bowman, "Cosmic Exemplarism," 185; Hayes, "Incarnation and Creation," 314.
[86]*The Soul's Journey into God* 2:1, 69.
[87]*Brev.* 2.12 (V, 230).
[88]*Hex.* 2.20 (V, 340).
[89]Bowman, "Cosmic Exemplarism," 197.
[90]Bonaventure, *The Major Legend*, in *FA:ED* 2, 596.
[91]See Bonaventure, "Five Feasts of the Child Jesus," trans. Timothy Johnson in *Bonaventure: Mystic of God's Word* (New York: New City Press, 1999), 139-52.

A Franciscan View of Creation

[92]On the integral relation between Christ and the cosmos see Zachary Hayes, "Christology-Cosmology," in *Franciscan Leadership in Ministry: Foundations in History, Theology, and Spirituality*, Spirit and Life: A Journal of Contemporary Franciscanism 7 (1997): 41-58.

[93]Hayes, "Bonaventure: Mystery of the Triune God," 68.

[94]Kenan B. Osborne, "Incarnation, Individuality and Diversity," *The Cord* 45.3 (1995): 22; John Duns Scotus, *A Treatise on God as First Principle*, trans. and ed. Allan B. Wolter (Chicago: Franciscan Herald Press, 1966), xvii.

[95]Osborne, "The Franciscan Intellectual Tradition," 70.

[96]Mary Beth Ingham, *Scotus for Dunces: An Introduction to the Subtle Doctor* (New York: The Franciscan Institute, 2003), pp. 56-7.

[97]Ingham, *Scotus for Dunces*, 264.

[98]Ingham, *Scotus for Dunces*, 266.

[99]Bonaventure *Sermo I Dom. II in Quad.* (IX, 215-219). Engl. trans. Zachary Hayes, "Christ, Word of God and Exemplar of Humanity," *The Cord* 46.1 (1996): 13.

[100]Richard Cross, *Duns Scotus* (New York: Oxford University Press, 1999), 33-9; Cyril L. Shircel, *The Univocity of the Concept of Being in the Philosophy of John Duns Scotus* (Washington, D.C.: Catholic University Press, 1942).

[101]Osborne, "The Franciscan Intellectual Tradition," 62.

[102]Ingham, *Scotus for Dunces*, 39-42.

[103]Francis of Assisi, "Admonition V," in *FA:ED* 1, 131.

[104]On the use of the term *haecceitas*, see Allan Wolter, "Scotus's Individuation Theory," in *The Philosophical Theology of John Duns Scotus*, ed. Marilyn McCord Adams (Ithaca: Cornell University Press, 1990), note 26, p. 76; also Wolter's *Duns Scotus' Early Oxford Lecture on Individuation* (Santa Barbara, CA: Old Mission, 1992).

[105]Wolter, *Scotus' Early Oxford Lecture on Individuation*, 25. We might note here that Scotus was trained at the University of Oxford, which held a more scientific (Aristotelian) approach to nature. Scotus likely acquired a scientific mentality through the influence of Robert Grosseteste, Roger Bacon and others. This attention to detail may also account for his particularity of words, which helped ground his views on individuality. This Franciscan attention to detail is very compatible with an empirical and scientific approach to nature but it is quite unlike that of Bonaventure who, trained at Paris, was imbued with a more mystical, sacramental understanding of creation.

[106]William Short, "Pied Beauty: Gerard Manley Hopkins and the Scotistic View of Nature," *The Cord* 45.3 (1995): 30.

[107]Short, "Pied Beauty," 32.

[108]Short, "Pied Beauty," 31.

[109]Gerard Manley Hopkins, as quoted in Short, "Pied Beauty," 31.

[110]Short, "Pied Beauty," 32.

[111]Hopkins, as quoted in Short, "Pied Beauty," 30.

[112]Pierre Teilhard de Chardin, *The Divine Milieu*, trans. William Collins (New York: Harper & Row, 1960), 66. As Teilhard de Chardin professed: "By virtue of the Creation and, still more, of the Incarnation, *nothing* here below is *profane* for those who know how to see."

[113]Teilhard de Chardin wrote: "The Christian knows that his function is to divinize the world in Jesus Christ," *The Divine Milieu*, 72.

[114]Mary Beth Ingham, "A Certain Affection for Justice," *The Cord* 45.3 (1995): 17.

[115]Ingham, "A Certain Affection for Justice," 17.

[116]Hayes, "Christ, Word of God and Exemplar of Humanity," 12.

Ilia Delio, O.S.F.

[117]Bonaventure, *De reductione artium ad theologiam* 20 (V, 324).

[118]As quoted by Short, "Pied Beauty," 35.

[119]Hayes, "Christ, Word of God and Exemplar of Humanity," 13.

[120]Keith Warner, "Out of the Birdbath: Following the Patron Saint of Ecology," *The Cord,* 48.2 (1998): 85.

SELECT BIBLIOGRAPHY

Allen, Paul M. and Joan deRis Allen. *Francis of Assisi's Canticle of the Creatures: A Modern Spiritual Path.* New York: Continuum, 1996.
Bodo, Murray. *The Threefold Way of Saint Francis.* New York: Paulist Press, 2000.
Cousins, Ewert H. "Francis of Assisi and Bonaventure: Mysticism and Theological Interpretation." In *The Other Side of God.* Ed. Peter L. Berger. New York: Anchor Press, 1981.
—. "Francis of Assisi: Christian Mysticism at the Crossroads." In *Mysticism and Religious Traditions.* Ed. Stephen Katz. New York: Oxford, 1983.
—. "Francis of Assisi: Nature, Poverty and the Humanity of Christ." In *Mystics of the Book.* Ed. R. A. Herrara. New York: Peter Lang, 1993.
Delio, Ilia. "The *Canticle of Brother Sun*: A Song of Christ Mysticism." *Franciscan Studies* 52 (1992): 1-22.
Doyle, Eric. *St. Francis and the Song of Brotherhood.* New York: Seabury Press, 1981. See reprint:: *St. Francis and the Song of Brotherhood and Sisterhood.* New York: Franciscan Institute Publications, 1997.
Gagnan, Dominique. "La Croix et La Nature Chez Saint François D'Assise." *Antonianum* 57 (1982): 609-705.
Hayes, Zachary. "Christ, Word of God and Exemplar of Humanity." *The Cord* 46.1 (1996): 3-17.
—. "Bonaventure: Mystery of the Triune God." In *The History of Franciscan Theology.* Ed. Kenan B. Osborne. New York: The Franciscan Institute, 1994.
Ingham, Mary Beth. *The Harmony of Goodness: Mutuality and Moral Living According to John Duns Scotus.* Quincy, IL: Franciscan Press, 1996.
—. *Scotus for Dunces: An Introduction to the Subtle Doctor.* St. Bonaventure, NY: The Franciscan Institute, 2003.
Osborne, Kenan B. "Incarnation, Individuality and Diversity." *The Cord* 45.3 (1995): 19-26.
Short, William. "Pied Beauty: Gerard Manley Hopkins and the Scotistic View of Nature." *The Cord* 45.3 (1995): 27-36.
Sorrell, Roger D. *St. Francis of Assisi and Nature: Tradition and Innovation in Western Christian Attitudes Toward the Environment.* New York: Oxford, 1988.

Vining, Timothy. "A Theology of Creation Based on the Life of Francis of Assisi." *The Cord* 40 (1990): 101-11.

Warner, Keith. "Out of the Birdbath: Following the Patron Saint of Ecology." *The Cord* 48.2 (1998): 74-85.

Wolter, Allan B., trans. and ed. *John Duns Scotus: A Treatise on God as First Principle*. Chicago: Franciscan Herald Press, 1966.